ATHENIAN DEMOCRACY

ATHENIAN DEMOCRACY

A. H. M. JONES

Late Professor of Ancient History in the
University of Cambridge

THE JOHNS HOPKINS UNIVERSITY PRESS
BALTIMORE

First published in paperback, 1977
Johns Hopkins Paperbacks edition, 1986

The Johns Hopkins University Press
701 West 40th Street, Baltimore, Maryland 21211

Library of Congress Cataloging-in-Publication Data

Jones, A. H. M. (Arnold Hugh Martin), 1904–1970.
Athenian democracy.
Bibliography: p.
Includes index.
1. Athens (Greece)—Politics and government.
2. Athens (Greece)—Social conditions.   I. Title.
JC79.A8J6   1986   320.938′5   86–45460
ISBN 0–8018–3380–9 (pbk.)

PREFACE

THE reprinting of collections of already published articles is in principle to be reprobated, but in this case there are extenuating circumstances. All the papers here collected deal with the same theme and are closely interlocked. Two, 'The Economic Basis of the Athenian Democracy' and 'The Athenian Democracy and its Critics', are out of print and very difficult to obtain. The fifth, 'How did the Athenian Democracy work'? (based on a course of lectures given at Cambridge in 1956), and the appendix on 'The Citizen Population of Athens during the Peloponnesian War' (expanded from a paper read to the Cambridge Philological Society in 1953), are here presented for the first time.

I have to thank the editors of *Past and Present*, the *Cambridge Historical Journal* and the *Economic History Review*, and the Syndics of the Cambridge University Press, for permission to republish the first, third, fourth and second articles respectively, and Sir Basil Blackwell for undertaking the publication.

I owe a debt of gratitude to various friends who have offered me criticisms and suggestions, including Mr. M. I. Finley, Mr. Guy Griffith, Mr. D. M. Lewis and Mr. Russell Meiggs. My special thanks are due to Mr. Geoffrey de Ste Croix, whose vigilant care has corrected many errors, and whose forthright arguments have sometimes caused me to alter my views.

I have reprinted the articles almost as they stood, only correcting some errors of fact, and making the references uniform and eliminating some redundant notes. There is as a result some overlapping and repetition, but it would have been difficult to remove this without recasting the whole, and I hope that readers will bear with it charitably.

A. H. M. JONES
Jesus College, Cambridge, June 1957

CONTENTS

I

THE ECONOMIC BASIS OF THE ATHENIAN DEMOCRACY

The Economic Basis of the Athenian Democracy[1]

PRIMA FACIE the Athenian Democracy would seem to have been a perfectly designed machine for expressing and putting into effect the will of the people. The majority of the magistrates were annually chosen by lot from all qualified candidates who put in their names, so that every citizen had a chance to take his turn in the administration. In the fifth century the military officers, of whom the most important were the ten generals, were elected by the assembly. In the fourth, when finance became a difficult problem, a few high financial officers were also elected. This was an inevitable concession to aristocratic principles: for the Greeks considered popular election to be aristocratic rather than democratic, since the ordinary voter will prefer a known to an unknown name—and in point of fact the generals usually tended to be men of wealth and family, though a professional soldier or two were usually members of the board in the fourth century. But the assembly, of which all adult male citizens were members, kept a strict control over the generals, who received precise instructions and departed from them at their peril. The assembly was in a very real sense a sovereign body, holding forty regular meetings a year and extraordinary sessions as required, and not merely settling general questions of policy, but making detailed decisions in every sphere of government—foreign affairs, military operations, finance.

The administrative lynch-pin of the constitution was the council of five hundred, annually chosen by lot from all the demes (wards or parishes) of Athens and Attica in proportion to their size, and thus forming a fair sample of the people as a whole. It had two main functions, to supervise and co-ordinate the activities

3

of the magistrates, and to prepare the agenda of the assembly. No motion might be put to the assembly unless the question had been placed on the order paper by the council and duly advertised; snap divisions were thus precluded. On uncontroversial issues the council usually produced a draft motion, which could however be freely debated and amended in the assembly by any citizen; in this way much formal business was cleared away. On controversial issues the council normally—and naturally in view of its composition—forebore to express an opinion, and merely put the question before the people, leaving it to any citizen to draft the motion during the actual debate. The presidents of the council and the assembly were chosen daily by lot from the council to preclude any undue influence from the chair.

Finally, as ultimate guardians of the constitution, there were the popular law courts. Juries were empanelled by lot for each case from a body of 6,000 citizens annually chosen by lot, and decided not only private cases but political issues. These juries as a regular routine judged any charges of peculation or malfeasance brought against magistrates on laying down their office; they decided the fate of any citizen accused of treason or of 'deceiving the people' by his speeches in the assembly; they could quash any motion voted in the assembly as being contrary to the laws, and punish its author. Political trials were frequent in Athens, and in the fourth century in particular the indictment for an illegal motion was constantly employed for political purposes, often on very technical grounds. The result was that the popular juries—in such cases sometimes thousands strong—tended to become a Supreme Court.

In general all citizens who were not expressly disqualified for some offence, such as an unpaid debt to the treasury, had equal political rights: in particular all could speak and vote in the assembly. For membership of the council and of the juries and probably for all magistracies there was an age qualification of 30 years. For offices, or at any rate some of them, there were also qualifications of property: but these were mostly moderate and, by the late fourth century, at any rate, and probably by the fifth, were in practice ignored.[2] To make the system work truly democratically it was further necessary that every citizen, however poor, should be able to afford the time for exercising his political rights, and from the time of Pericles pay was provided for this purpose.[3] Magistrates were paid at varying rates according to the nature of their duties;[4] members of the council received 5 obols a day by the fourth century—the rate may have been lower in the fifth;[5] and members of the juries were given a subsistence allowance of 2 obols, raised in 425 B.C. to 3.[6] Finally from the beginning of the fourth century citizens who attended the assembly—or rather the quorum who arrived first, for a limited sum of money was allocated to each assembly—were paid a subsistence allowance of 1, then 2, then 3 obols.[7] Later the rate was more liberal, 1 drachma for ordinary days, $1\frac{1}{2}$ for the ten standing meetings when the agenda was heavier.[8]

Two charges have been brought against the Athenian democracy, one both by ancient and by modern critics, the other in recent times only. The first is that the pay, which was an essential part of the system, was provided by the tribute paid by Athens' allies in the Delian League, and that the democracy was therefore parasitic on the empire: the second, that Athenians only had the leisure to perform their political functions because they were supported by slaves—the democracy was in fact parasitic on slavery.

To the first charge there is a very simple answer, that the democracy continued to function in the fourth century when Athens had lost her empire; the Second Athenian League, which lasted effectively only from 377 to 357, was never a paying proposition, the contributions of the allies by no means covering the cost of military and naval operations. And not only did the democracy continue to function, but a new and important form of pay, that for attendance in the assembly, was introduced early in the century. This being so it is hardly worth while to go into the financial figures, particularly as there must be many gaps in our calcula-

tions. The magistrates numbered about 350 in the later fourth
century, and, if they received on an average 1 drachma a day,
the annual bill would be 21 talents.[9] The council, if all the members were paid for every day of the year, would have cost rather
under 26 talents a year, but if councillors, like jurors, were paid
for actual attendance, the bill would be considerably less, since
sessions were not held every day and many members did not
attend regularly.[10] Assembly pay cannot be calculated as we do
not know how large the quorum was. The major item was the
6,000 jurors for whom Aristophanes[11] budgets 150 talents a year,
presumably by the simple method of multiplying 3 obols by
6,000 jurors by 300 court days (the courts did not sit on the
forty or more assembly days[12] nor on the numerous festivals).[13]
This is a theoretical maximum, for the whole 6,000 were not
empanelled in juries on every court day—Aristophanes' jurors
rise at dead of night to queue for their tickets.[14] As against this,
the internal revenue of Athens, apart from imperial receipts, can
be inferred to have been in the range of 400 talents a year in the
fifth century.[15] Since other peace-time expenditure was minimal,
pay was thus amply covered by internal income at this period.
In the fourth century the revenue dropped considerably; Demosthenes indeed stated that earlier in the century it amounted to only
130 talents.[16] He is perhaps thinking of the regular income from
taxes and rents, excluding receipts from fines, confiscations and
court fees, which were a considerable proportion of the whole.[17]
Even so, we know that in the first half of the fourth century it
was at times a tight squeeze.[18] By 340, however, the regular
revenue had risen to 400 talents again, and things were easy.[19]

   That Athens profited financially from her empire is of course
true. But these profits were not necessary to keep the democracy
working. They enabled Athens to be a great power and to
support a much larger citizen population at higher standards
of living. One oligarchic critic emphasises the casual profits
incidental on Athens' position as an imperial city; the imperial
litigation which brought in more court fees, the increased cus-

toms revenue, the demand for lodgings, cabs and slaves to hire.[20] Advocates and politicians made money by pleading the legal cases of the allies, and promoting measures in their favour. But these were chicken-feed compared with the solid benefits of empire, the tribute amounting to 400 talents a year and other imperial income raising the annual total to 600 talents,[21] and the acquisition of land overseas, mainly by confiscation from rebellious allied communities or individuals.[22]

The land was utilised either for colonies, which were technically separate states, but being composed of former Athenian citizens were virtually overseas extensions of the Athenian state, or for cleruchies, that is settlements of Athenians who remained full citizens, liable to Athenian taxation and military service, though in practice they naturally would rarely exercise their citizen rights at Athens. Both types of settlement were normally manned from the poorer citizens. Most will have come from the lowest property class, thetes, who possessed property rated under 2,000 drachmae and were liable only for naval service or as light-armed troops on land. The allotments were (in the one case where figures are given) of sufficient value to qualify the owner to rank as a zeugite, liable to military service as a heavy-armed infantry-man or hoplite. By her colonies and cleruchies Athens raised more than 10,000 of her citizens from poverty to modest affluence, and at the same time increased her hoplite force by an even larger number, the cleruchs with their adult sons serving in the ranks of the Athenian army and the colonists as allied contingents.[23]

The tribute was partly spent on the upkeep of a standing navy, partly put to reserve. Pericles is stated to have kept sixty triremes in commission for eight months in the year,[24] and he maintained a fleet of 300 in the dockyards.[25] The dockyards must have given employment to an army of craftsmen, as well as to 500 guards,[26] and the crews of the cruising triremes would have numbered 12,000 men, paid a drachma a day[27] for 240 days in the year. Not all the dockyard workers will have been citizens, nor all the naval ratings, but many thousands of Athenian thetes enjoyed regular well-paid employment thanks to the empire. Of the money put to reserve a part, probably 2,000 talents,[28] was spent on public works, notably the Parthenon and the Propylaea, which again, as Plutarch explains,[29] gave employment to the poorer classes. The remainder formed a war fund of 6,000 talents, which was ultimately spent during the Peloponnesian war on pay to hoplites and sailors.[30]

In response to the favourable economic conditions provided by the empire the population of Athens seems to have risen by leaps and bounds during the half-century between the Persian war (480-479) and the opening of the Peloponnesian war (431). The figures are unfortunately very incomplete and not altogether certain, but the general picture is clear enough; they refer to citizens liable to military and naval service, that is males between 20 and 60. At Salamis (480) the Athenians manned 180 triremes,[31] which required 36,000 men. As Attica had been evacuated and no army was mustered this figure probably represents the whole able-bodied population including resident aliens, so that the citizens may be reckoned at about 30,000. At Artemisium, earlier in the same year, the Athenians, supplemented by the population of the little city of Plataea, had manned 127 triremes[32] (25,400 men, perhaps 20,000 Athenians). As an invasion of Attica was expected the hoplites were probably held in reserve and only thetes served in the fleet. At Plataea (479) 8,000 Athenian hoplites fought,[33] but a large fleet was simultaneously in commission, which will have carried perhaps 2,000 marines of hoplite status: for Marathon (490) Athens had mustered 9,000 hoplites.[34] These figures suggest a total population of 30,000 citizens, a figure given elsewhere by Herodotus,[35] divided 1 : 2 between hoplites and thetes. At the opening of the Peloponnesian war there were over 20,000 citizen hoplites on the muster rolls. The rise will have been due partly to the general rise in prosperity which enabled many thetes, who owned little or no land, to acquire sufficient house property, slaves or cash capital to qualify as hoplites; but mainly

to the grant of allotments of land to thetes in the cleruchies.[36]
For the thetic class we have no reliable figures, for the large fleets
which Athens commissioned at this period were certainly manned
not only by citizens but by resident aliens and by foreigners
drawn from the cities of the empire.[37] But if, as Plutarch suggests,[38] the sixty ships kept regularly in commission during peace
time were largely manned by citizens, the crews of these, together with sundry standing land forces (1,600 archers and 500
shipyard guards, for instance[39]) and the 6,000 jurors, of whom a
large proportion were probably thetes, would account for 20,000
men. There were also workers employed in the shipyards, on
public works and in private industry, but many of these may have
been seasonal, spending the summer rowing and doing other
work in the winter. Despite the rise of many thousands into the
hoplite class, the thetes must have certainly maintained and probably considerably increased their numbers. Otherwise it would
be hard to account for the radical tone of the fifth century democracy, and the predominance, noted with disfavour by oligarchic
critics, of the 'naval masses' in its councils.

The Peloponnesian war caused great losses both by battle
casualties and by the plague: 1,000 hoplites fell at Delium[40] and
600 at Amphipolis,[41] and 2,700 hoplites and 130 triremes carrying
perhaps 13,000 citizen sailors, if half the crews were Athenians,
were sent to Sicily,[42] of whom only a remnant ever saw Athens
again, while in the plague 4,700 men of hoplite status and an
uncounted number of thetes perished.[43] Towards the end of the
war (411) there seem to have been only 9,000 hoplites resident in
Attica,[44] and after the war the cleruchs were all dispossessed. In
322 the hoplite class still numbered only 9,000 despite a revival
of prosperity. By that date the thetes numbered only 12,000.
Other evidence suggests that both figures were about the same
earlier in the century.[45] The loss of the empire and the fall of
Athens in 404 must have compelled many thousands of citizens,
dispossessed cleruchs and unemployed sailors and dockyard
workers, to emigrate or take service as mercenaries abroad. A

general decrease in prosperity caused the population to sink to a level well below that of the Persian wars, and in particular reduced the thetic class. Hence the increasingly bourgeois tone of the fourth century democracy.

The second charge against the Athenian democracy, that it was parasitic on slavery, is more difficult to answer with any certainty. It will be as well first to make plain the elements of the problem. The Athenians, like all Greek peoples, regarded themselves as a kinship group, and citizenship depended strictly on descent (always on the father's side and, by a law passed in 451 and re-enacted in 403, on the mother's side also) and not on residence, however long. The population of Attica therefore consisted not only of citizens but of free aliens, mainly immigrants who had settled permanently and often lived at Athens for generations, but also including freed slaves and persons of mixed descent; and of slaves, mainly imported but some home-bred. It is unhistorical to condemn the Athenian democracy because it did not give political rights to all residents of Attica; it was the democracy of the Athenian people. It is however relevant to enquire whether the Athenian people was a privileged group depending on the labour of others. Sparta might be called technically a democracy (though the hereditary kings and the council of elders balanced the power of the people) inasmuch as the whole body of Spartiates chose the ephors, in whose hands the government effectively lay, but the Spartiates were a body of rentiers supported by native serfs, the helots, who far outnumbered them. Was the Athenian democracy of this order? The resident aliens (metics) do not concern us here. They made a great contribution to Athenian prosperity, particularly in the fields of industry, commerce and banking—indeed they seem to have dominated the two latter. They were voluntary immigrants and could leave when they wished (except in time of war). That so many domiciled themselves permanently in Attica—a census taken at the end of the fourth century showed 10,000 metics as against 21,000 citizens—is a testimony to their liberal treatment. They enjoyed full civil (as opposed to political) rights, except that they could not own land—hence their concentration on industry and commerce—and were subject to all the duties of citizens, including military and naval service and taxation at a slightly higher scale. They were a contented class, and many demonstrated their loyalty to their adoptive city by generous gifts at times of crisis.[46]

What of slaves? Here it will be as well to clear up another misconception. It is often stated, mainly on the authority of Plato and Aristotle, that 'the Greeks' considered manual work degrading. Now it is true that gentlemen like Plato and Aristotle despised workers and justified their contempt by asserting that manual work deformed the body and the soul. But that this was the attitude of the average poor Greek there is no evidence. An anecdote recorded by Xenophon[47] probably gives a better insight into his point of view. Eutherus, who has lost his overseas estates as a result of the war, has been reduced to earning his living by manual labour. Socrates asks what he will do when his bodily strength fails and suggests that he find a job as a rich man's bailiff. Eutherus is horrified at the suggestion—'I could not endure to be a slave . . . I absolutely refuse to be at any man's beck and call'. What the Athenian thete objected to was not hard work—incidentally his main military duty in the fifth century was rowing in the galleys, a task in most later civilisations considered fit only for infidel slaves or convicts—but being another man's servant. He would work as an independent craftsman or at a pinch as a casual labourer,[48] but he would not take even a black-coated job as a regular employee; we find that such highly responsible posts as the manager of a bank or the foreman overseer of a mine are filled by slaves or freedmen of the owner.[49]

Is it true, as we are still too often told, that the average Athenian, in the intervals between listening to a play of Sophocles and serving as a magistrate, councillor or juror, lounged in the market place, discussing politics and philosophy, while slaves toiled to support him? Contemporary critics of the democracy did not think so. Plato's Socrates, analysing the people in a democracy, divides them into the drones, that is the active politicians and their cliques of supporters, and the mass of the people 'who support themselves by their labour and do not care about politics, owning very little property; this is the largest and most powerful element in a democracy when it is assembled'.[50] Xenophon's Socrates, rebuking Charmides for his shyness at addressing the assembly, asks if he is afraid 'of the fullers among them or the shoemakers or the carpenters or the smiths or the peasants or the merchants or the shopkeepers: for the assembly is composed of all of them'.[51] Aristotle, analysing the people (that is the mass of poor citizens) in different cities, classifies them as craftsmen, shopkeepers, seamen of various kinds—fishermen, ferrymen, sailors on merchantmen or warships—and casual day labourers and those who have little property so that they can enjoy no leisure.[52]

Slaves were employed in many capacities—as domestic servants, as clerks and agents in commerce and banking, in agriculture, and in industry and mining. All well-to-do Athenian families had several servants, and no doubt wealthy men kept large households of a dozen or more—precise figures are lacking—but the domestic servant probably did not go very far down the social scale. A man for whom Lysias wrote a little speech does indeed roundly assert that everyone has slaves; but he is trying to convince the jury that it is contrary to public policy to encourage slaves to inform against their masters.[53] In comedy domestic slaves appear when dramatically convenient, even in the poorest households,[54] but this evidence is suspect: comedy was written after all by well-to-do authors, and slaves provided a variety of stock comic turns. It has been argued that because in the fifth century every hoplite took with him an attendant to carry his food and kit, and was allowed a drachma a day by the State on his account (in addition to his own drachma[55]), every hoplite must have owned an able-bodied male slave. Those hoplites who owned suitable slaves certainly used them for this purpose,[56] but there is no evidence that every hoplite's attendant was his own slave. The high rate of the State allowance, on the contrary, is only explicable on the assumption that many hoplites would have to hire a man for the purpose, and Thucydides' inclusion of the baggage carriers with the light-armed among the Athenian casualties at Delium implies that they were citizens.[57] More significant than these uncertain inferences is a remark by Demosthenes, who, castigating the harshness with which Androtion and Timocrates collected the arrears of war tax, pictures them 'removing doors and seizing blankets and distraining on a servant girl, if anyone employed one'.[58] Now the payers of war tax can be estimated to have numbered only about 6,000 out of a population of 21,000.[59] If not all of them had a domestic servant, one may hazard that under a quarter of the population enjoyed that luxury.

Commerce and banking need not detain us, as the numbers were small. In agriculture, too we hear little of slaves. The property of large landowners did not normally consist of a single great estate, but of several farms scattered over Attica.[60] Some of these farms were let to free tenants, Athenian or metic;[61] one at least—the home farm—would be worked by a minimum staff of slaves, supplemented by hired labour;[62] for it was uneconomic in a seasonal trade like agriculture to maintain all the year round enough slaves to cope with peak demands. The hired labour was sometimes supplied by slave gangs, leased from a contractor to do a particular job, such as to get in the harvest or the vintage;[63] but it often consisted of free persons—in one of his private speeches Demosthenes remarks that many citizen women were driven by poverty to work in the harvest.[64] Shepherds seem normally to have been slaves,[65] but the politician Phrynichus is alleged to have been one in his poverty-stricken youth.[66] How far down the scale of wealth the use of agricultural slaves went it is difficult to say, but the greater part of Attica was probably occupied by peasant farmers too poor to afford them. Of the 6,000 citizens who paid war tax, a large number were, as Demosthenes puts it, 'farmers who stinted themselves, but owing to the maintenance of their children and domestic expenses and other public demands fell into arrears with their war tax'.[67] These were the men who sometimes could not afford a single domestic servant, and certainly did not maintain a farm hand; they would fall into the class which Aristotle described as using the labour of their wives and children through lack of slaves.[68] Below them were the remaining 3,000 of the hoplite class who did not qualify for war tax, and will have owned property to the value of between 25 and 20 minae.[69] These were quite poor men; Demosthenes introducing a poor hoplite witness apologises to the jury—'he is poor, it is true, but not a rascal'[70]—and the wealthy Mantitheus, when his deme mustered for a call-up, found that many of his fellow demesmen were embarrassed for journey money, and distributed 30 drachmae to each.[71] A farm worth 20 minae would, on the basis of the single land price recorded, comprise about 5 acres, and would bring in if let only about 160 drachmae a year in rent, not enough to feed, let alone clothe, a single man; it can only have supported a family if worked by family labour.[72]

In industry, and particularly mining, slaves were employed on a larger scale. The wealthy Nicias in the fifth century is said to have owned 1,000 slaves, whom he let out to a mining contractor at 1 obol a day, the contractor feeding and clothing them and replacing casualties; two rich contemporaries are said to have owned 600 and 300 respectively whom they exploited in a similar way.[73] In the fourth century another mine concessionaire owned thirty slaves,[74] which was probably a more usual number. Well-to-do Athenians also normally invested a small proportion of their wealth in slave craftsmen, who either worked together in a factory, or independently, paying their owner a fixed sum and keeping for themselves whatever they earned beyond it. The largest factory of which we hear, the shield factory of the brothers Lysias and Polemarchus, numbered nearly 120 men;[75] but this is quite exceptional, and is due to the fact that the owners were metics, who could not invest in land, and that the thirty years of the Peloponnesian war had naturally led to a boom in armaments. In the fourth century Pasion the banker also ran a shield factory as a side-line; it brought in a net revenue of a talent a year, and must have contained over sixty men; Pasion again was a metic, until he was rewarded with the citizenship for his public services,[76] and he was the richest man in Athens of the time—he had before he died acquired land to the value of 20 talents besides his bank and factory. Demosthenes' father was also exceptional in owning two factories, thirty-two knife makers and twenty bed makers, with a capital value of nearly 6½ talents (4 talents in slaves and 2½ talents in raw materials in stock) out of a total fortune of 14 talents, the rest of which was in cash and investments with the exception of his house and furniture.[77] We hear of some others in the fifth century whose wealth was entirely invested in slaves; Isocrates' father rose to affluence from the profits of a group of flute-makers,[78] and Xenophon makes Socrates cite five contemporaries, including a miller, a baker and cloakmaker, who lived comfortably on the earnings of their slaves.[79] More usually rich Athenians seem to have distributed their capital between land, house property, some cash investments and a dozen or so slave craftsmen. Socrates, asking a high-class prostitute where her money came from, suggests (ironically) land, house property or craftsmen as typical sources of income.[80] Timarchus inherited, besides land and houses, nine or ten shoemakers, who paid him 2 obols a day each:[81] Leocrates owned bronzesmiths to the value of 35 minae (about a dozen, that is [82]): Ciron, besides an estate worth a talent, and two houses, owned a few rent-paying slaves, valued with three domestic slaves and the furniture at 13 minae:[83] Euctemon possessed a farm, a house, a baths, and a brothel and wineshop and some craftsmen.[84]

These facts and figures concern the well-to-do families who could afford to pay a professional speech writer to compose a plea in their mutual litigation about their inheritances, and who normally belonged to the 1,200 richest families enrolled on the trierarchic register. How far humbler folk owned industrial slaves it is very difficult to say. Xenophon in one passage speaks of those who could buying slaves as fellow workers,[85] which might suggest that a craftsman sometimes bought a man and trained him as an apprentice; and a poor cripple, pleading for his public assistance of 1 obol a day, complains that he is getting old and his children are too young to support him (a rather unlikely conjunction of pleas) and that he is too poor to buy a slave to carry on his work.[86] This may suggest that a craftsman who bought a slave and trained him was looking forward to retiring on his earnings. But, as Aristophanes recognised, the greater part of the work in industry as in agriculture was done by poor citizens. Addressing them Poverty declared in the *Plutus*: 'If wealth should gain his sight again and distribute himself equally, no one would practise a craft or skill. And when you have lost both of these, who will work as a smith or a shipwright or a tailor or a wheel-wright or a shoemaker or a bricklayer or a launderer or a tanner or plough the land or harvest the crops, if you can live in idleness and neglect all this work?'

We have no reliable evidence for the total number of slaves in Attica at any time. For the late fourth century we have two figures, which, if we could rely on them, would be startling. The Byzantine lexicon of Suidas[87] cites Hypereides (probably in connection with his proposal to free the slaves after the battle of Chaeronea in 338 B.C.) as speaking of 'more than 150,000 from the silver mines and over the rest of the country.' Athenaeus,[88] who wrote at the end of the second century A.D., quotes Ctesicles, a chronicler of unknown date, as stating that at the census held by Demetrius of Phaleron (317-07) 400,000 slaves were registered. These are, as Beloch[89] has convincingly demonstrated, quite impossible figures, and must have been corrupted in the course of their transmission to the late sources in which we read them. To turn to more reliable if less explicit evidence, according to Thucydides more than 20,000 slaves, mainly skilled men, escaped during the ten years' occupation of Deceleia by the Spartans;[90] these would probably be in the main miners and agricultural slaves, but would include many city workers, since the sixteen miles of city walls cannot have been so completely patrolled as to prevent escapes.

Xenophon declares that the mines could provide employment for many more than 10,000, as those—if any—who remembered what the slave tax used to fetch before the Deceleian war could testify (he was writing sixty years later).[91] But whatever their numbers their distribution is fairly clear. They were owned in the main by the 1,200 richest families and in decreasing numbers by the next 3,000 or so. It is unlikely that any slaves were owned by two-thirds to three-quarters of the citizen population. The great majority of the citizens earned their living by the work of their hands, as peasant farmers, craftsmen, shopkeepers, seamen and labourers; so contemporary witnesses state, and so the detailed evidence, so far as it goes, suggests. In only one occupation was slave labour predominant, in mining, and even here, contrary to common belief, some citizens worked. Xenophon, advocating that the State acquire a large body of slaves to be leased to the citizens for use in the mines, suggests that not only will existing contractors add to their manpower but that 'there are many of those who are themselves in the mines who are growing old, and many others, both Athenians and aliens, who would not or could not work with their hands, but would gladly make their living by supervising'.[92] In one of the Demosthenic speeches we meet a man who boasts 'In earlier times I made a lot of money from the silver mines, working and toiling myself with my own hands': he had struck lucky and was now one of the 300 richest men in Athens.[93]

That the poorer citizens lived on State pay for political services is, even for the fourth century, when the system was most fully developed, demonstrably false. A man could only be a councillor two years in his life, and could hold none of the magistracies chosen by lot for more than one annual tenure.[94] He could by attending the assembly—and getting there in time to qualify for pay—earn a drachma on thirty days and $1\frac{1}{2}$ drachmae on ten days in the year. On some festivals—the number varied according to the state of the exchequer—he could draw his theoric payment of 2 obols.[95] On other days, if lucky enough to be successful in the annual ballot for the 6,000 jurors, he could queue in hopes of being empanelled on a jury and earning 3 obols, just enough to feed himself. At this rate a bachelor without dependants could barely with consistent good luck scrape a living; for a man with a family it was quite impossible.

The majority of the citizens were then workers who earned their own livings and whose political pay served only to compensate them in some measure for loss of working time. Agricultural and industrial slaves in the main merely added to the wealth of a relatively small rentier class, whose principal source of income was land; this same class employed most of the domestic slaves. It only remains to ask how far the Athenian State drew its revenue, directly or indirectly, from slaves. The State owned a certain number of slaves. Most famous are the 1,200 Scythian archers who policed the assembly and the law courts and enforced the orders of the magistrates.[96] There were a number of others ranging from the workers in the mint to the city gaoler and the public slave *par excellence* who had custody of the public records and accounts. Athens thus ran her police force and her rudimentary civil service in part by slave labour—the clerks of the magistrates were mostly salaried citizens.[97] There was apparently a tax on slaves, known only from the mention in Xenophon cited above,[98] but it can hardly have been an important item in the revenue to receive so little notice. The mines, which were mainly exploited by slave labour, also brought in revenue to the State, but less than might have been expected seeing that concessionaires sometimes made large fortunes. The mines flourished in the fifth century, from their first serious exploitation in 483 till the Spartan occupation of Deceleia in 413. They then went through a prolonged bad period till the 330s, when they were again in full swing. We have no figures for the fifth century. In the fourth we have a full record of one year's concessions (367-6), when the sums paid totalled 3,690 drachmae, and a partial record of a later year—probably 342-1—when the revenue came to about 3 talents.[99] There was probably a royalty payment of one twenty-fourth in addition to the prices paid for concessions.¹⁰⁰ It is somewhat mysterious where the 400 talents of Athenian revenue came from, but a negligible proportion of it arose even indirectly from slave labour.

The charge brought by fifth-century oligarchic critics (and thoughtlessly repeated by many modern writers), that the Athenian democracy depended for its political pay on the tribute of the subject allies, was brought to the test of fact when Athens lost her empire in 404 B.C., and was proved to be a calumny when the democracy continued to pay the citizens for their political functions out of domestic revenues. The modern charge that the Athenian democracy was dependent on slave labour was never brought to the test, since the Athenians never freed all their slaves. This is not surprising, for slavery was an established institution, which most people accepted without question as 'according to nature,' and to abolish it would have meant a wholesale disregard of the rights of property, which the Athenians throughout their history were careful to respect. It is more surprising that on some occasions of crisis motions for a partial or wholesale freeing of slaves were carried. In 406 all male slaves of military age were freed and granted the citizenship to man the ships which won the battle of Arginusae.¹⁰¹ After the expulsion of the Thirty in 403, Thrasybulus, the left-wing leader of the restored democracy, carried a measure, later quashed as illegal by the moderate leader Archinus, to free and enfranchise all slaves who had fought for the democracy.¹⁰² In 338, after the defeat of Chaeronea, the left-wing politician Hypereides proposed and carried a motion to free all (able-bodied male) slaves to resist the Macedonians; this motion was again quashed as illegal by a conservative politician.¹⁰³

These facts suggest that there was no bitterness between the mass of the citizens and the slaves, but rather a sense of fellow-feeling. This was a point which shocked contemporary Athenian oligarchs. The 'Old Oligarch' speaks bitterly of the insolence of slaves at Athens, and complains that it is illegal to strike them— the reason, he explains, is that the people are indistinguishable in dress and general appearance from slaves, and it would be easy to strike a citizen by mistake.[104] The moderate oligarch Thera- menes is careful to assure his colleagues among the Thirty that he is not one of 'those who think there would not be a good demo- cracy until slaves and those who through poverty would sell the city for a drachma participate in it'.[105] Plato mocks at the excess of freedom in the democracy, in which 'men and women who have been sold are no less free than their purchasers'.[106]

Though the Athenians treated their slaves with a humanity which was exceptional according to the standards of the time, they never abolished slavery, and the charge that Athenian demo- cracy was dependent on their labour was never brought to the test of fact. But had Hypereides' motion been allowed to stand, and extended to slaves of all ages and both sexes, it would not seem, on the basis of the evidence cited earlier in this article, that its effects would have been catastrophic. All wealthy and well-to- do citizens (or rather their wives and unmarried daughters) would have been incommoded by having to do their own housework. A very small number of wealthy or comfortably off men who had invested all their money in mining and industrial slaves would have been reduced to penury, and a larger number, but still a small minority, would have lost the proportion of their income which derived from industrial slaves, and would have had to let their farms instead of cultivating them by slave labour. A number of craftsmen would have lost their apprentices and journeymen. But the great majority of Athenians who owned no slaves but cultivated their own little farms or worked on their own as crafts- men, shopkeepers or labourers would have been unaffected.

II

THE ATHENS OF DEMOSTHENES

The Athens of Demosthenes

DEMOSTHENES' aims and policy have often been discussed, but his biographers have rarely paid much attention to the Athenians to whom he spoke. We are left with the general impression that, in contrast with the patriotic orator, they were an idle, cowardly, pleasure-loving crew, who would not fight or pay their taxes, but preferred to draw their dole at home, paying—or rather failing to pay—mercenaries to fight their battles. Is this estimate just? It is the picture which appears to emerge from Demosthenes' speeches, which, with those of contemporary orators, afford almost all the evidence available. This evidence I propose to examine afresh.

'Pay war tax' (εἰσφέρετε) and 'serve yourselves in the army' (αὐτοὶ στρατεύεσθε) are the two key-notes of Demosthenes' appeals to the people. Let us first examine the war tax. It is a highly technical and controversial subject, and I hope that you will excuse me if I am somewhat dogmatic. The questions which I wish to answer are: Was it, as is generally believed, a progressive tax? How many people paid it, and what was the limit of exemption? How much money was actually raised?

The *eisphora* was a war tax, raised by decree of the people as occasion demanded, and took the form of a capital levy. For this purpose a census of property was held in 378/7 B.C., in which according to Polybius 'the total assessment' (τὸ σύμπαν τίμημα) of Attica was valued at 5750 talents;[1] Demosthenes speaks of 'the assessment of the country' (τὸ τίμημα . . . τῆς χώρας) as being in his day 6,000 talents, and reckons levies as percentages of this sum —1 per cent. will bring in 60 talents, 2 per cent. 120 talents and so

forth.[2] Now Polybius clearly thought that the 'assessment'
represented the total capital (land, houses and other property) of
the country—he ignores the fact that it excludes properties below
the exemption limit—and represented its real value. Demosthenes, however, in one passage of his first speech against Aphobus[3] uses 'assessment' in another sense: 'three talents is the assessment of fifteen talents', he says (πεντεκαίδεκα ταλάντων γὰρ
τρία τάλαντα τίμημα), and he implies that for smaller fortunes
the proportion was less than one-fifth. On this passage, together
with an obscure citation in Pollux,[4] has been built the theory
that the 'assessment' was not the real value of a man's property,
but the taxable value, and that the taxable value was a higher
proportion of the real value for the rich than for the poor, so
that the *eisphora* was the only known progressive tax of
antiquity.

This theory involves very serious difficulties. In the first place
it seems very perverse that even the richest should be assessed at
one-fifth of their capital; the natural course would have been to
assess them at the whole, and scale down the assessment of the
poorer classes only. In the second place the theory conflicts with
a contemporary inscription,[5] a lease in which the tenant is to pay
54 drachmae a year rent and the *eisphorae*, if any, 'according to
the assessment, viz. 7 minae' (κατὰ τὸ τίμημα καθ᾽ ἑπτὰ μνᾶς);
the rent works out at about 8 per cent. if 7 minae is the real value
of the property, but is absurd if the real value is five or more
times that sum. It also makes the 'total assessment' of Attica
absurd. Six thousand talents is perhaps rather a low sum, but it
excludes, we must remember, thousands of small properties below the exemption limit, and, as frequent allusions in the orators
show,[6] concealment of wealth and under-assessment were the
rule rather than the exception. On the other hand it is quite
impossible that the value of Athenian property assessable for
tax can have been not merely five times 6,000 talents, but much
more. 'Assessment' is then used in two senses—to denote the real
value in the inscription and in the phrase 'the assessment of the

country' and as Demosthenes uses it in the first speech against Aphobus. And moreover the tax was levied on the assessment in the first sense of real value, or Demosthenes' calculation that a 1 per cent. levy will yield 60 talents is nonsense. Demosthenes must be using the word in an untechnical way in the passage in which he states that the 'assessment' of 15 talents is 3 talents for the largest fortunes.

Now Demosthenes alludes several times to this 1:5 ratio, but in all the other passages[7] he uses different phraseology: 'they expected me to pay this tax' (ταύτην ἠξίουν εἰσφέρειν τὴν εἰσφοράν), he says, or 'to pay 500 drachmae per 25 minae' (κατὰ τὰς πέντε καὶ εἴκοσι μνᾶς πεντακοσίας δραχμὰς εἰσφέρειν), as if his guardians put him down to pay one-fifth of his fortune as tax. Of course tax was never levied at this fantastic rate—actually during the ten years of his minority Demosthenes paid 18 minae on the 15 talents at which he was assessed.[8] What do Demosthenes' phrases mean? Mr. Meiggs[9] has recently suggested that the one-fifth is a ceiling, the highest sum which the richest class could be asked to pay as the total of all their tax payments during their lifetime; for the poorer categories of taxpayers this ceiling would be lower. *Eisphora* was then levied as a given percentage of the real value of all taxable properties, and was not a progressive tax: but if successive levies came to a total of say a twentieth (the actual figures are unknown) of their capital, men of the poorest class could claim exemption, while men of the richest class would go on paying till a fifth of their capital was exhausted.

The theory is attractive in that it gives a meaning to Demosthenes' phraseology and tallies with Greek ways of thinking: they tended to regard a man's fortune as a static sum, ignoring income, and to set off against it the total of his payments on trierarchies, liturgies and war tax.[10] But to put such a system into practice would have involved calculations of great complexity; for in fact fortunes were not static, but rose and fell by inheritances and investment of surplus income on the one hand, and payment of dowries and sales of assets on the other. I find it hard to believe that so complicated a system could have worked and I submit an alternative explanation of Demosthenes' words, which was suggested to me by my former pupil, Mr. de Ste Croix.[11] In one passage Demosthenes states that his guardians made him president (ἡγεμών) of his symmory not on a small valuation but on so high a one as to pay 500 drachmae on 25 minae.[12] Now the presidents with the second and third men (δεύτεροι and τρίτοι) of the symmories later constituted the Three Hundred,[13] who advanced the tax to the State (οἱ προεισφέροντες), subsequently recovering it from the other members of their symmories. May it not be that this system existed from the beginning of the symmories, and that it was liability for this prepayment of tax (προεισφορά) which was scaled up to one-fifth of the payer's fortune according to his wealth?

There are difficulties in this view also. There were in 357 arrears amounting to about 14 talents on the 300-odd talents which had been demanded in the previous twenty years.[14] Some of these arrears may have been due from members of the Three Hundred: it is perhaps significant that of the individual debtors mentioned by Demosthenes two are known to have been trierarchs,[15] and must therefore have been fairly wealthy men, who might have been enrolled in the Three Hundred. But at any rate half of the total arrears was made up out of quite small sums, scarcely any according to Demosthenes over 1 mina;[16] which implies 400 or 500 debtors. How did all these taxpayers still owe money to the treasury if their tax had been advanced by the Three Hundred? They might still owe money to members of the Three Hundred, but not to the State.

Two answers are possible. It may be that the 'prepayment' was a device designed for use in emergencies only, and was rarely or not at all employed in the twenty years in question. Or again the original function of the Three Hundred may have been not to prepay but to guarantee or underwrite the tax of their symmories; this is perhaps suggested by the use of 'pay' (εἰσφέρειν) and not 'prepay' (προεισφέρειν) in connection with the Three

Hundred in the earliest reference to them.[17] In that case the guarantee may well never have been enforced, for there was little enthusiasm to collect the tax when once the emergency which had demanded it was past.[18]

The second difficulty is that when in 362 an emergency levy was raised to finance a naval expedition, the people decreed that the members of the council should nominate on behalf of their demes persons who were members of the deme or owned land in it to advance the levy to the State.[19] Here the Three Hundred are entirely ignored, and it has generally been assumed that they did not yet exist. It was, on the usual view, the emergency of 362 which first called for a 'prepayment' and the procedure described above was a first experiment, which led to the establishment of the standing body of Three Hundred.

One objection to this view is that, in a speech delivered a few years before, Isaeus[20] alludes to the Three Hundred as an established institution connected with the *eisphora*. A second is that about 376 (that is directly after the establishment of the symmory system) Demosthenes was made president of his symmory, though a child of 7, because of his wealth: the post of president, that is, was not executive but carried financial responsibility from the first. It seems a necessary inference that the Three Hundred comprising the presidents, second and third men of the 100 symmories were from the beginning financially responsible for the tax due from their groups, either by prepaying or by underwriting it. Indeed this would seem to be the whole point of the symmory system.

It was not then because the Three Hundred did not yet exist that the people in 362 decreed that persons be nominated *ad hoc* in each deme to prepay the tax. It may be that a 'prepayment' had been levied very recently, and that the Three Hundred had claimed that their hands were already full; if there had been a levy in the previous year they could, since the 'prepayment' was a liturgy, have legally claimed exemption.[21] Or alternatively it may be that the symmory system through long disuse had become so disorganised that when a sudden emergency arose it had to be abandoned and *ad hoc* measures adopted. In favour of this view it may be noted that the emergency legislation ignores not only the Three Hundred but, it would seem, the whole symmory system: for it is implied that the collection was made not by symmories but by demes.[22] It may even be that this levy was not a normal *eisphora*, but a special tax on some other basis, substituted for it either because the capacity of the war taxpayers was temporarily exhausted or because the machinery for assessing and collecting a war tax was seriously out of gear. The speaker uses the words προεισφέρειν and προεισφορά, but these may not be technical terms but mean merely 'to prepay a levy'. On the other hand he alludes to the magistrates who were in charge of the levy as 'the collectors of the military fund' (οἱ τὰ στρατιωτικὰ εἰσπράττοντες),[23] which suggests a special military levy rather than a regular war tax.

The object of this long argument has been to prove that the *eisphora* was not a progressive tax, that is, that all liable to it paid the same proportion of their capital, whether they were rich or poor. Now for my second question, How many citizens paid? That the number was large is implied by Demosthenes' language in several passages; he speaks for instance of the mass of the people (τῷ πλήθει τῷ ὑμετέρῳ) as being exhausted by payment of war tax.[24] A rather more precise answer is, I think, possible. There were, it is generally agreed, 100 war tax symmories as against 20 trierarchic symmories.[25] The 20 trierarchic symmories, which were modelled on those of the *eisphora* , comprised 1,200 persons, at 60 per symmory.[26] The 100 war tax symmories on the same basis will have included 6,000 persons. What was the exemption limit? Demosthenes several times alludes to 25 minae as a basic assessment unit—'to pay 500 drachmae per 25 minae' (κατὰ τὰς πέντε καὶ εἴκοσι μνᾶς πεντακοσίας δραχμὰς εἰσφέρειν)[27] and, on one occasion, even more significantly assumes it as such —'you assessed me to pay 5 minae' (πέντε μνᾶς συνετάξατ' εἰσφέρειν), meaning to pay one-fifth.[28] This suggests that 25 minae was the minimum taxable capital. This would accord with what other figures we have. In 322 B.C. Antipater, limiting the franchise to citizens owing over 2,000 drachmae (or 20 minae), found that there were 9,000 who qualified.[29] If there were 9,000 persons who owned more than 20 minae each, there might well be about 6,000 who owned more than 25 minae.

Finally, how much war tax was actually levied? In his speech against Androtion Demosthenes tells us that the levies between 377 and 357 totalled perhaps 300 talents or a little more;[30] this works out at 0.25 per cent. per annum on the assessment of 6,000 talents. Demosthenes during his ten years' minority (376-366) paid 18 minae on his assessment of 15 talents,[31] which works out at about 0.2 per cent. per annum. This is on capital, of course, but reckoning income as 10 per cent. of capital, which is about right taking land and money together, levies during this period, which was full of wars, represented only a 2 to 2½ per cent. income tax, or in modern terms 5d. to 6d. in the pound. We may therefore with some justification be amused when Xeno-phon speaks of the Athenians during this very time as 'worn out by levies of war tax' (ἀποκναιόμενοι χρημάτων εἰσφοραῖς).[32] But taxation is a matter of habit—our great-grandfathers were outraged by an extra penny in the pound—and the Athenians never could form the habit of paying war tax since it was an occasional payment and, when it came, relatively heavy—Demos-thenes speaks of 1 per cent. and even 2 per cent. as normal,[33] and these are equivalent to an income tax of 2s. and 4s. in the pound. And before we blame the Athenians too loudly we should re-member that there was no personal allowance, wife's allowance or children's allowance to soften the blow to the poor man with a large family. Demosthenes is probably justified in invoking the jurors' sympathy for 'the farmers who pinch and scrape, but owing to the cost of bringing up their children and domestic expenses and other public demands have fallen into arrears of war tax.'[34] It must have meant much pinching to bring up a family on a farm worth 25 minae. One litigant, indeed, states that 'my father left me and my brother property of only 45 minae each, and it is not easy to live on that'.[35] On the basis of the single fourth-century figure that we possess for the price of land,[36] a farm worth 25 minae would have comprised about 7 acres—without stock, implements, house or furniture. If let at the rate of 8 per cent. which seems to have been normal,[37] it would have brought in a rent of 200 drachmae a year; and bare food for a single man, without counting clothes, shoes or any extras, cost 180 drachmae.[38] The proprietor of such a holding normally of course worked it himself with the aid of his family, and would make a larger income than the rental value, but even so little enough to feed a family.

An ill-adjusted system of war tax meant then that while the rich got off relatively very lightly, the mass of poor taxpayers were really embarrassed by even an occasional small levy, and were very reluctant to vote one. Actually very little was raised. How then did Athens pay for her wars? For the answer one may turn to Isocrates' panegyric on Timotheus.[39] Timotheus' great merit, it appears, was that he was a very cheap general. He received only 13 talents from the treasury for his great campaign round the Peloponnese in which he won Corcyra in 375. Apollodorus gives a vivid picture of his financial straits two years later, when he had to mortgage his estates and borrow right and left to keep his sixty ships together,[40] and Iphicrates, his successor, had to hire out his rowers as agricultural labourers in the intervals between operations.[41] For the campaign which resulted in the capture of Samos in 365 Timotheus received no public funds, and he financed the capture of Potidaea and other Thraceward cities in the following year from the contributions of the local allies.

These facts affect Demosthenes' second slogan, hoplite service. The Athenians cannot be accused of cowardice. They turned out for campaigns in the good old fifth-century style in Boeotia, Euboea, the Peloponnese and even as far afield as Thessaly. In 369 they raised a levy *en masse* in support of Sparta against Thebes;

6,000 fought at Mantinea in 362; 5,000 foot and 400 horse at Thermopylae in 352. For Chaeronea there was a levy *en masse*, and 5,000 foot and 500 horse fought in the Lamian war.[42] The Athenians did not object to fighting. What they were afraid of may be deduced from the scheme for a small standing army which Demosthenes put forward in the *First Philippic*. The Athenian element is to serve for a fixed period, not a long one at that, by a regular system of reliefs;[43] and the State, he insists, must make financial provision for paying them a ration allowance at the meagre rate of 2 obols a day[44]—by way of comparison ephebes (young men doing their military training in Attica) were allowed 4 obols a day for their food under Lycurgus' régime,[45] and even public slaves got 3 obols a day.[46] They will make up the balance, Demosthenes euphemistically hopes, 'from the war'.

In two other passages Demosthenes implies that hoplites were normally expected to keep themselves. In the *de Falsa Legatione*[47] he estimates the cost of the expedition to Thermopylae at 200 talents, 'if you count the private expenditure of those who served', and in the *First Olynthiac*[48] he asserts that 'if you had to serve abroad yourselves for only thirty days, and take what you would need on service from the produce of the country—while no enemy was in the country, I mean—those of you who are farmers would I think suffer a heavier loss than all you have spent on the war up to date'.

What the Athenian hoplite dreaded, then, was being shipped off to Macedonia and left there to starve for an indefinite period, while the farm or the business at home went to rack and ruin. Things were very different from the good old days of the fifth century, when a hoplite got 2 drachmae a day.[49] And it must be remembered that many hoplites were quite poor men; the qualification is generally, and probably correctly, believed to have been property to the value of 2,000 drachmae[50]—roughly 5 acres and a cow. Demosthenes in the *Meidias* is quite apologetic for introducing to the jury a poor hoplite witness—'he is poor may be, but

not a rascal' (πένης μὲν ἴσως ἐστίν, οὐ πονηρὸς δέ γε)—a
curious remark in a speech devoted to abuse of the rich man
Meidias.[51] Lysias' client Mantitheus, when his deme assembled
for the muster, found that many of his poorer fellow hoplites
could not raise their journey money and organized a subscription
to supply each with 30 drachmae.[52]

The same considerations applied a *fortiori* to naval service,
which Demosthenes also frequently urged on the citizens, since
it was thetes who served in the fleet. It may be noted that at this
period Athens could not rely on volunteers to row her triremes,
but conscription was regularly employed.[53] If one reads Apollodorus' speech against Polycles one realises why. Gone were the
days of a drachma a day;[54] for two months only did the men get
any pay, for the remaining year and five months only rations,
and even the ration money was often short, and failed altogether
for the return voyage.[55] For a man with a wife and family to
keep this meant disaster, and it is little wonder if, as Apollodorus
says, whenever a trireme put back to Athens in the middle of the
year, large numbers deserted and the rest refused to sail again
unless they were given something to provide for their families
(εἰς διοίκησιν τῶν οἰκείων).[56]

Lack of public funds naturally increased the expenses of trierarchs also. In 373 Timotheus made his sixty trierarchs each
advance 7 minae to feed their crews[57]: he being a rich man was
able to cover this advance by mortgages on his estates, but other
trierarchs were less fortunate; Apollodorus had to borrow freely
from his father's correspondents overseas.[58] The main vice of the
trierarchy, however, was the faulty working of the symmory
system. Trierarchic symmories were introduced in 357 B.C.[59]
because the trierarchy or syntrierarchy, whereby one or two men
were responsible for the upkeep of a trireme for one year, was
found too heavy a burden on some of the persons liable. But
no rules seem to have been laid down for sharing the expenses
within the symmory and the general practice was that all members
paid an equal share. This resulted, as Demosthenes explains in

the *Meidias* and the *de Corona*, in the richest members, who could
well afford to be sole trierarchs two or three times over, paying
one-sixteenth of a trierarchy, while the same amount was paid
by the poorer members of the 1,200 who could ill afford it.[60]
Demosthenes' first scheme of reform, set out in the speech on the
symmories, was ill conceived; he proposed, it is true, to make
payments proportional to property, but he also suggested spread-
ing the burden yet wider over the whole body of war taxpayers.[61]
The result would have been to make the tricrarchy a supplementary war tax, with all its unfairness. Later Demosthenes grasped
the real point, and threw the whole burden of the trierarchy on
the 300 richest citizens in proportion to their means, so that some
performed two trierarchies.[62]

You have no doubt been long waiting for me to mention the
theoricon, which occupies a larger space in Demosthenes' commen-
tators than in his speeches, and was of greater political than financial importance—as Demosthenes himself says, 'The sum of
money about which you are debating is small, but the habit of
mind which goes with it is important'.[63] The fund consisted of
the annual surplus of regular revenue over peace-time expenses
(τὰ περιόντα χρήματα τῆς διοικήσεως)—in war time the surplus
went by law to the war fund (τὰ στρατιωτικά)[64]—and was
used for making distributions to the citizens at the rate of 2
obols a head on some festival days.[65] According to Demosthenes
even the well-to-do drew it,[66] let us then suppose that of the
21,000 citizens[67] as many as 18,000 actually took the money.
The cost would then be 1 talent per day.

The number of distributions varied according to the state of
the fund. One lexicographer mentions a drachma as the total in
395—394 B.C.;[68] that is three distributions were made, probably
for the three days of the Dionysia. Another lexicographer speaks
of payments for the Dionysia and the Panathenaea[69]—six days in
all. Hypereides[70] mentions a man who impersonated his son who
was abroad, and was fined a talent for the sake of 5 drachmae; this
sum he may well have drawn over several years. But assuming

that 5 drachmae represents a year's takings, that is that distributions were made on as many as fifteen days, the annual expenditure would be 15 talents, or one-quarter of a 1 per cent. *eisphora.*

The only evidence that large sums were involved is an anecdote in Plutarch,[71] that when the Athenians were eager to launch a fleet to assist the rebels against Alexander, Demades quenched their ardour by stating that the money would have to come from a sum which he had reserved for a distribution at the rate of 50 drachmae a head for the feast of the Choes. If this anecdote has any historical basis, I am inclined to link it with another, according to which Lycurgus (very uncharacteristically) distributed the confiscated estate of one Diphilus to the people at the rate of 50 drachmae (or some say 1 mina) a head.[72] The incident will presumably have taken place in 331, when King Agis was taking the field, and Demades and Lycurgus seem to have been working together to keep Athens out of the war. This payment of 50 drachmae was then not a normal theoric distribution, but a special bonus, arising from a windfall to the treasury.

Be that as it may, all the evidence shows that in the middle of the fourth century the *theoricon* must have been financially very small beer, and Demosthenes was rather foolish to make himself and his policy unpopular by trying to transfer it to the war fund even in peace time. When the revenue was as low as 130 talents a year, it was no doubt irritating to see even half a dozen talents squandered, and Demosthenes fell into Eubulus' trap. Later, when the revenue had risen to 400 talents, he changed his mind, and in the *Fourth Philippic* he argues—somewhat sophistically—in favour of the *theoricon.*[73] Politically the *theoricon* was, as Demades put it, 'the glue of the democracy' (ἡ κόλλα τῆς δημοκρατίας),[74] because all classes found it useful. The poor, which would include not only the thetes but a substantial proportion of the hoplites, naturally found even so tiny a dole very acceptable, since it enabled them to enjoy their festivals with a clear conscience. To the rich it was a valuable political weapon for the policy of peace or appeasement which they favoured. Eubulus could threaten not only *eisphorae*, which affected only 6,000 voters, but the transfer of the *theoricon* to the war fund, which affected all the citizens, if the assembly would not vote for the Peace of Philocrates.[75] Meidias could say, 'Do you expect me to pay war tax for you while you receive distributions?'[76] A large part of the *Fourth Philippic* is devoted to combating the argument of the well-to-do citizens that they cannot be expected to pay war tax and perform trierarchies if the poor draw their dole.[77]

It is somewhat paradoxical that the leaders of the peace party should have been a group of the very wealthy men who, owing to the inefficiency of the Athenian financial machine, contributed least in proportion to their means to war expenses. But, this being so, this very inefficiency played into their hands, for war inflicted disproportionate hardship on every other class. Even the well-to-do, the less wealthy of the 1,200 members of the trierarchic symmories, bore an unfair proportion of naval expenses. The more modest war taxpayers were hard pressed to pay their share of the levy. The humble hoplites and the thetes looked forward with dread to being called up for prolonged unpaid foreign service in the army and the fleet, and moreover had to sacrifice their theoric doles. It was these last who really suffered the most by war, yet it was they who, if roused to action, voted for war. On Alexander's death, Diodorus[78] tells us, the men of property (οἱ κτηματικοί) urged that Athens stay quiet, and it was the masses (τὰ πλήθη) who responded to the appeals of the orators of the war party, and declared the Lamian war, in which Athens played so prominent and so creditable a part.

It is understandable that the masses should have required some rousing to vote for war, when it meant such hardship for them. What is less easy to understand is why, once involved in war, they did not vote levies of tax which would have provided them with adequate pay for hoplite and naval service. The war taxpayers numbered only about 6,000, well under a third of the total citizen body of 21,000, and one might have expected the majority of the assembly to vote eagerly for a tax which they would not have to pay. In this connection it is worth noting the language that Demosthenes uses. He never urges the poor to soak the rich; on the contrary he appeals to the assembly to pay tax themselves. In every passage save one the war taxpayers are alluded to in the second person,[79] and the one exception is significant. It is in the speech on the symmories, where Demosthenes is curbing a war-like assembly and deprecating a levy; here he says, 'Suppose *you* want *us* to pay an 8⅓ per cent. tax?'[80] The inference seems to be that, contrary to general belief, the average assembly was attended mainly by the relatively well-to-do citizens, so that the war taxpayers were, if not in a majority, a substantial part of the audience, and that it was only at moments of crisis—the speech on the symmories was delivered to combat a war scare that the Persian king was about to attack Athens—that the poorer classes came in force and might outvote those who would have to pay the tax.

If this was so in the assembly, it was even more markedly so in the law courts, where so many political issues were ultimately decided by way of the indictment for illegal proceedings (γραφὴ παρανόμων). We generally picture the law courts as manned by the very poor, eager to earn their 3 obols, but the language of Demosthenes and his contemporaries is hardly consistent with this view. The *Meidias*, with its constant appeal to prejudice against wealth, might seem at first sight to support it. But Meidias is represented as very rich, and moreover ostentatious, a bully and a shirker of his public obligations, and it is note-worthy that Demosthenes finds it necessary to apologise for introducing a really poor witness, the arbitrator Strato, who is a hoplite.[81] The speech might well have been delivered to an audience of well-to-do propertied persons (οἱ εὔποροι or οἱ τὰς οὐσίας ἔχοντες are phrases of commendation in other speeches), who would probably dislike an insolent rich man (πλούσιος is consistently a term of abuse) more than would the very poor. In the *Androtion* and the *Timocrates* Demosthenes depicts the woes of the humbler payers of war tax in a way which he evidently expects to excite the sympathy of his audience—a really poor audience would not have felt very indignant at Androtion's distraining his victims' single maidservants when they had none themselves.[82] The *Leptines* is a very strange speech to deliver to a poor audience. Not a word is said about the effect of the law on the masses, in their capacity of either audiences to the spectacles produced by the choregi or of dancers in the choruses.[83] Leptines' plea was that his law would relieve the (comparatively) poor from the burden of liturgies by abolishing the exemptions of the rich, and Demosthenes tries to prove that the quashing of the law will not adversely affect the class who had to undertake liturgies:[84] his speech must have been addressed to a jury drawn mainly from that class. Even more revealing is a remark in Deinarchus' speech against Demosthenes,[85] where he appeals to any jurors who were members of the Three Hundred when Demosthenes passed his trierarchic law to tell their neighbours how he was bribed to amend it. Such an appeal would have been ridiculous unless members of the Three Hundred, the richest men in Athens, frequently sat on juries.

Upon reflection this is not unnatural. The greatest political issues and the fate of statesmen were decided in the courts. Would it not be prudent for leading politicians to get their supporters to enrol in the 6,000 jurors? They were not obliged to empanel themselves every day for minor cases, but could turn out in force when a *cause célèbre* was to be tried. And there was probably little competition for enrolment as a juror; a working man could not keep a family on 3 obols a day—he could only just feed himself— and he could earn three times as much even by casual unskilled labour.[86] Why the poor did not attend assemblies, where the pay was better—a drachma or even 9 obols—is more difficult to explain. They perhaps found the intricacies of politics as run by the professionals (οἱ πολιτευόμενοι) baffling, and were frustrated by finding every decree they passed taken to the courts and quashed under the indictment for illegal proceedings.

This analysis has, I hope, helped to explain against what heavy odds Demosthenes was battling in his great struggle for Athenian democracy, and at the same time given you a more sympathetic understanding of the Athenian people to whom he spoke.

III

THE ATHENIAN DEMOCRACY AND ITS CRITICS

The Athenian Democracy and its Critics[1]

IT IS curious that in the abundant literature produced in the greatest democracy of Greece there survives no statement of democratic political theory. All the Athenian political philosophers and publicists whose works we possess were in various degrees oligarchic in sympathy. The author of the pamphlet on the 'Constitution of the Athenians' preserved among Xenophon's works is bitterly hostile to democracy. Socrates, so far as we can trace his views from the works of Xenophon and Plato, was at least highly critical of democracy. Plato's views on the subject are too well known to need stating. Isocrates in his earlier years wrote panegyrics of Athens, but in his old age, when he wrote his more philosophical works, became increasingly embittered against the political régime of his native city. Aristotle is the most judicial in his attitude, and states the pros and cons, but his ideal was a widely based oligarchy. With the historians of Athens, the same bias is evident. Only Herodotus is a democrat, but his views have not carried much weight, partly because of his reputation for naïveté, and partly because his explicit evidence refers to a period before the full democracy had evolved. Thucydides is hostile: in one of the very few passages in which he reveals his personal views he expresses approval of a régime which disfranchised about two-thirds of the citizens, those who manned the fleet on which the survival of Athens depended. Xenophon was an ardent admirer of the Spartan régime. Aristotle, in the historical part of his monograph on the Constitution of Athens, followed—rather uncritically—a source with a marked oligarchic bias. Only the fourth-century orators were democrats; and their speeches, being concerned with practical political issues—mostly

41

of foreign policy—or with private litigation, have little to say on the basic principles of democracy, which they take for granted.[2]

The surviving literature is certainly not representative of Athenian public opinion. The majority of Athenians were proud of their constitution and deeply attached to it. The few counter-revolutions—in 411, 404, 322 and 317—were carried out by small extremist cliques, in 411 after a carefully planned campaign of deception and terror, in the other three cases with the aid of a foreign conqueror, and all were short-lived, being rapidly overwhelmed by the mass of the citizens. Nor was it only the poor majority, who most obviously benefited from the system, that were its supporters. Most of the great statesmen and generals of Athens came from wealthy families, and a substantial number from the nobility of birth; the leaders of the popular risings which unseated the oligarchic governments of 411 and 403 were men of substance.

Since, however, the majority were mute—in the literature which has survived—it is not an easy task to discern what they considered the merits of democracy to be, or, indeed, on what principles they thought that a good constitution should be based. Democratic political theory can only be tentatively reconstructed from scattered allusions. For the basic ideals of democracy the best source is the series of panegyrics on Athens. The most famous of these, Pericles' Funeral Speech, as recorded by Thucydides, is also the most instructive; its peculiarities of diction and its general tone, which is in conflict with Thucydides' own outlook, suggest that it is a fairly faithful reproduction of what Pericles really said. There is an early fourth-century Funeral Speech attributed to Lysias, which contains some useful material. Little for our purposes can be drawn from Isocrates' *Panegyricus* and *Panathenaicus*. A curious document of this class is the skit on a Funeral Speech contained in Plato's *Menexenus*, which seems close enough to type to be used—with reservations—as a statement of democratic principles. To these documents, which too often only repeat banal generalities, may be added *obiter dicta* in the political and forensic speeches of the orators, when they appeal to some general principle. Among these may be included some political speeches in Thucydides, which, though placed in a Sicilian setting, doubtless are modelled on Athenian prototypes. Another important source is the actual constitution of Athens, from whose rules general principles can sometimes be deduced. But our most valuable evidence comes from the criticisms of adversaries, which are so much more fully reported than any-thing from the democratic side. This evidence, though copious, is tricky to evaluate and must be used with caution. We must distinguish criticism on points of principle, where a democrat would have accepted his opponent's statement of the democratic point of view as correct, and would have argued that the principle or institution criticised was in fact a good one; and criticism on points of practice, which a democrat would have endeavoured to rebut, arguing that the accusations were untrue, or alternatively that the abuses alleged were regrettable but accidental and remedi-able defects of democracy.

It is the object of this paper to reconstruct from these sources democratic political theory and then to determine how far in practice the Athenian people lived up to its principles. The procedure will be to take up the various lines of criticism ad-vanced by oligarchic critics, and to work out on what lines demo-crats would have answered them, using for this purpose the scattered evidence outlined above. The criticisms of the philosophical writers will be analysed first, and then those of the historians—or rather of Thucydides, who alone demands discussion. This dis-tinction in the source of the criticism corresponds with a division in subject-matter, for the philosophers confine their attacks almost entirely to the internal working of democracy, while Thucydides is primarily interested in Athenian foreign and imperial policy.

The first and most basic charge brought by the philosophers against democracy is best expressed by Aristotle in his character-istic terse direct style: 'in such democracies each person lives as he likes; or in the words of Euripides "according to his fancy". This is a bad thing.'[3] This is no isolated text. Aristotle returns to the point elsewhere.[4] Isocrates in the *Areopagiticus*[5] declares that in the good old days it was not the case that the citizens 'had many supervisors in their education but as soon as they reached man's estate were allowed to do what they liked', and urges that the Areopagus should recover its alleged pristine pᵣwer of controlling the private lives of all the citizens. Plato in the *Republic*[6] complains that under a democracy 'the city is full of liberty and free speech and everyone in it is allowed to do what he likes. . . each man in it could plan his own life as he pleases'. He then enlarges on the deplorable results of this, that the citizens are various, instead of conforming to one type, and that foreigners and even women and slaves are as free as the citizens.[7]

An Athenian democrat would no doubt have demurred at the last charge, though admitting with some pride that foreigners and slaves were exceptionally well treated at Athens,[8] but he certainly gloried in the accusation of liberty. Freedom of action and of speech were the proudest slogans of Athens, and not only political but personal freedom; as Pericles says in the Funeral Speech,[9] 'we live as free citizens both in our public life and in our attitude to one another in the affairs of daily life; we are not angry with our neighbour if he behaves as he pleases, we do not cast sour looks at him, which, if they can do no harm, cause pain'. Freedom of speech was particularly prized.[10] As Demosthenes[11] says, 'in Sparta you are not allowed to praise the laws of Athens or of this state or that, far from it, you have to praise what agrees with their constitution', whereas in Athens criticism of the democracy was freely permitted. One only has to read the works of Isocrates, Plato and Aristotle to see that this is true. The condemnation of Socrates is an apparent exception to the rule, but as Xenophon's[12] account of the matter shows, the real gravamen of the charge against Socrates was that, of his pupils, Alcibiades had done more than any other one man to ruin Athens in the recent war, and Critias had been the ruthless ringleader of the

Thirty, who had massacred thousands of Athenians a few years before.

The second main charge against democracy is most neatly stated by Plato:[13] that 'it distributes a kind of equality to the equal and the unequal alike'. The same point is made by Isocrates,[14] who distinguishes 'two equalities; one allots the same to every one and the other what is appropriate to each'. and alleges that in the good old days the Athenians 'rejected as unjust the equality which considers the good and the bad worthy of the same rights, and chose that which honours each according to his worth'. Aristotle[15] argues similarly, though he is justifiably sceptical about the criterion according to which rights are to be scaled; in democracy freedom is the criterion, that is, all free men are equal, and this is in Aristotle's view unjust, but so in his opinion are the only practical alternative criteria, wealth or birth.

Democrats in general approved of the egalitarian principle.[16] Demosthenes in one passage[17] argues that what makes all citizens public spirited and generous is 'that in a democracy each man considers that he himself has a share in equality and justice'. and in another[18] praises a law forbidding legislation directed against individuals as being good democratic doctrine, 'for as everyone has an equal share in the rest of the constitution, so everyone is entitled to an equal share in the laws'. The Athenians were not, however, either in theory or in practice, absolute egalitarians, but drew a distinction between different political functions. On one point they admitted no compromise—equality before the law; as Pericles[19] says, 'in their private disputes all share equality according to the laws'. This to us elementary principle needed emphasis, for Plato's friends in the Thirty, when they drew up a new constitution, ordained that only the 3,000 full citizens were entitled to a legal trial and that all others might be summarily executed by order of the government.[20] It was secured in the Athenian constitution not only by the right of every citizen to seek redress in the courts, but by the character of the courts, which consisted of large juries drawn by lot from the whole body of the citizens.

The Athenians also attached great importance to the equality of all citizens in formulating and deciding public policy. This was secured by the right of every citizen to speak and vote in the assembly, and by the composition of the council of Five Hundred, which prepared the agenda of the assembly; this body was annually chosen by lot from all the demes of Attica. Here democratic principle came into conflict with the oligarchic view, developed at length by Plato, that government was an art, demanding the highest skill, and should therefore be entrusted to a select few. On this question Aristotle, whose ideal was a broadly based oligarchy, whose members would not all be experts, took issue with Plato, and the arguments which he uses are applicable to a fully democratic régime, and probably drawn from democratic theory. In the first place[21] he argues that, though each individual in a large assembly may be of poor quality, the sum of their virtue and wisdom taken together may exceed the virtue and wisdom of a select few, just as dinners provided by joint contributions may be better than those provided by one rich host. His second argument[22] is rather more cogent. Politics, he suggests, is one of those arts in which the best judge is not the artist himself but the user of the product. The householder is a better judge of a house than the architect, the steersman of a rudder rather than the carpenter, the eater of a meal rather than the cook. A third justification for democratic practice is put into the mouth of Protagoras by Plato[23] in a passage which so well illustrates the tone of the Athenian assembly that it is worth quoting in full. Socrates is expressing his doubts as to whether political wisdom is teachable.

I, like the other Greeks (he says), think that the Athenians are wise. Well, I see that when we gather for the assembly, when the city has to do something about buildings, they call for the builders as advisers and when it is about ship construction, the shipwrights, and so on with everything else that can be taught and learned. And if anyone else tries to advise them, whom they do not think an expert, even if he be quite a gentleman, rich and aristocratic, they none the less refuse to listen, but jeer and boo, until either the speaker himself is shouted down and gives up, or the sergeants at arms, on the order of the presidents, drag him off or remove him. That is how they behave on technical questions. But when the debate is on the general government of the city, anyone gets up and advises them, whether he be a carpenter or a smith or a leather worker, a merchant or a sea-captain, rich or poor, noble or humble, and no one blames them like the others for trying to give advice, when they have not learned from any source and have had no teacher.

Protagoras' reply is in mythological form. Zeus when he created men gave various talents to each, but to all he gave a sense of decency and fair play, since without them any society would be impossible.

So, Socrates, (he concludes) that is why the Athenians and the others, when the debate is about architecture or any other technical question, think that few should take part in the discussion, and if anyone outside the few joins in, do not tolerate it, as you say—rightly in my opinion. But when they come to discuss political questions, which must be determined by justice and moderation, they properly listen to everyone, thinking that everyone shares in these qualities—or cities wouldn't exist.

The Athenians went yet further in their egalitarian principles in that they entrusted the routine administration of the city to boards of magistrates chosen by lot. This aroused the irony of Socrates,[24] who declared that 'it was silly that the rulers of the city should be appointed by lot, when no one would be willing to employ a pilot or a carpenter or a flautist chosen by lot'. It is a proof of the poverty of our information on democratic theory that no reasoned defence of this cardinal institution, the lot, has survived. The nearest thing to it is a comic passage in a private speech of Demosthenes[25] where Mantitheus, pleading against the assumption of his name by his half-brother, raises the hypothetical case that both might put in their names for the ballot for an office or the council, and that the name Mantitheus might be drawn. There would have to be a lawsuit 'and we shall be deprived of our common equality, that the man who wins the ballot holds office: we shall abuse one another and the cleverer speaker will hold the office'. It is implied that the lot was employed to give every citizen an equal chance, without regard to wealth, birth or even popularity or eloquence. This may seem to be carrying principle to extremes, but Socrates' comment is not altogether fair. It was not 'the rulers of the city' who were chosen by lot, but officials charged with limited routine duties, for which little more than 'a sense of decency and fair play' was required. Furthermore, it must be remembered that a magistrate had to pass a preliminary examination, which was, it is true, usually formal, but gave his enemies an opportunity for raking up his past;[26] was liable to be deposed by a vote of the assembly taken ten times a year;[27] and after his year was subject to a scrutiny in which his accounts were audited and any citizen could charge him with inefficiency or abuse of authority.[28] It is unlikely that many rogues or nincompoops would expose themselves to these risks.

Athenian democrats did not believe that all should share alike in the important offices, whose holders to some extent controlled policy. Pericles,[29] after affirming the equality before the law of all citizens, goes on: 'but in public esteem, when a man is distinguished in any way, he is more highly honoured in public life, not as a matter of privilege but in recognition of merit; on the other hand any one who can benefit the city is not debarred by poverty or by the obscurity of his position.' This point is even more strongly put in the mock panegyric in the *Menexenus*:[30]

For in the main the same constitution existed then as now, an aristocracy, under which we now live and have always lived since then. A man may call it democracy, and another what he will. But in truth it is an aristocracy with the approval of the majority. We have always had kings: sometimes they were hereditary, sometimes elective. In most things the majority is in control of the city, and bestows office and power on those whom it thinks to be the best. No one is rejected for weakness or poverty or humble birth, nor honoured for their opposites, as in other cities. There is one criterion: the man who is thought to be wise and good holds power and rule.

These principles were embodied in the Athenian constitution, whereby all the important magistrates—the ten generals, who not only commanded the army and the fleet but exercised a general control over defence and foreign policy, the other military commanders, and in the fourth century the principal financial magistrates—were elected by the people; a procedure which could be regarded as aristocratic.[31] In fact, the Athenian people were rather snobbish in their choice of leaders.[32] The 'Old Oligarch'[33] sneeringly remarks, 'they do not think that they ought to share by lot in the offices of general or commander of the horse, for the people knows that it gains more by not holding these offices itself but allowing the leading citizens to hold them'. Xenophon[34] records the complaints of Nicomachides, an experienced soldier, that he has been beaten in the elections for the generalship by a rich man who knows nothing about military affairs. Demosthenes, a strong democrat, rakes up Aeschines' humble origins in a fashion which we should hardly consider in good taste, but apparently did not offend an Athenian jury. 'We have judged you, a painter of alabaster boxes and drums, and these junior clerks and nobodies (and there is no harm in such occupations, but on the other hand they are not deserving of a generalship) worthy of ambassadorships, generalships and the highest honours'.[35]

Besides the lot the other instrument whereby the Athenians secured the effective political equality of the citizens was pay. The 6,000 jurors, the council of 500 and the 350 odd magistrates were all paid for their services at various rates; it may be noted that elective magistrates—the military commanders and ambassadors—were paid, and at higher rates than the ordinary magistrates chosen by lot,[36] so that the claim that poverty was no barrier to political power was justified. During the fourth century citizens who attended the assembly—or at least a quorum who arrived first—were also paid. The philosophers objected to this practice. Aristotle[37] criticises it precisely because it fulfilled its purpose of enabling the poor to exercise their political rights. It may, however, be doubted if by his day it was fully effective.

The assembly and the juries seem, from the tone in which the orators address them, to have consisted predominantly of middle-class citizens rather than of the poor,[38] and there is evidence that the council also was mainly filled by the well-to-do.[39] The real value of the State pay had, owing to the progressive rise of prices, sunk considerably by the latter part of the fourth century, and the poor probably preferred more profitable employment. Plato[40] also objects to State pay: 'I am told', he says, 'that Pericles made the Athenians idle and lazy and garrulous and avaricious by first putting them on State pay.' This is an oft-repeated accusation but has very little substance. In a population which never sank below 20,000 adult males and probably reached twice that figure at its peak, the council and the magistracies did not provide employment except on rare occasions; a man might not hold any magistracy more than once, or sit on the council more than twice in his life.[41] Assemblies were held only on forty days in the year.[42] It was only as a juror that a citizen could obtain more or less continuous employment, and here the rate of remuneration was so low—half a labourer's wage in the fifth century and a third in the late fourth, in fact little more than bare subsistence[43]—that in the fifth century, if the picture drawn in Aristophanes' *Wasps* is true, it attracted only the elderly, past hard work, and in the early fourth century, when economic conditions were worse, according to Isocrates, the unemployed.[44]

The third main criticism of democracy comes from Aristotle,[45] that in its extreme (that is, Athenian) form 'the mass of the people (or the 'majority') is sovereign instead of the law; this happens when decrees are valid instead of the law'. It is not entirely clear what Aristotle means by this. He appears here and elsewhere to conceive of the law as an immutable code, laid down by an impartial legislator, against which the will of the citizens, assumed always to be self-interested, should not in an ideal State be allowed to prevail. He may therefore be objecting to any legislation by decision of the majority—or, for that matter, by any constitutional procedure. But this meaning seems to slide into another, that in an extreme democracy the majority in the assembly habitually overrides the existing laws, however established, by arbitrary executive action in particular cases, acting, as he puts it, like the traditional Greek tyrant.

The doctrine of the immobility of law was naturally favoured by oligarchs, who were generally conservative, or, when they wanted to alter the law, professed to be restoring an 'ancestral constitution'. Democrats, who more often wished to change things, might have been expected to work out a more progressive theory. Some thinkers in the fifth century did indeed propound the doctrine that the law was the will of the sovereign. Socrates, according to Xenophon,[46] defined law as 'what the citizens have by agreement enacted on what must be done and what avoided', and was quite prepared to admit that what the citizens enacted they could revoke, just as having declared war they could make peace. Xenophon[47] also reports a no doubt imaginary conversation between Pericles and Alcibiades, in which the former defined law as 'what the mass of the people (or "the majority"), having come together and approved it, decrees, declaring what must and what must not be done'. Led on by Alcibiades he extends this definition to oligarchies and tyrannies, declaring that what the sovereign body or person decrees is law. Asked by Alcibiades what then is violence and lawlessness, Pericles replies 'when the stronger does not persuade the weaker but compels him by force to do what he wants'. This enables Alcibiades after suitable leading questions about tyrants and oligarchies, to ask: 'Would what the whole mass of the people, overpowering the holders of property, enacts without persuading them, be violence rather than law?' Pericles at this point tells Alcibiades to go away and play, leaving the ambiguity in his theory of law unresolved. In the fourth century Demosthenes[48] enunciates a similar view in one passage, asserting that 'the laws lay down about the future (he is denouncing retrospective legislation as undemocratic) what must be done, being enacted by persuasion as they will benefit their users'. Some democrats then conceived of law as the considered will of the majority, adding the rider that the majority should persuade the minority and consider the interests of all.

In general, however, democrats tended like Aristotle to regard the laws as a code laid down once for all by a wise legislator, in their case Solon, which, immutable in principle, might occasionally require to be clarified or supplemented. These were the terms of reference given to the legislative commission set up after the restoration of the democracy in 403.[49] and the standing rules governing legislation show the same spirit. At no time was it legal to alter the law by a simple decree of the assembly. The mover of such a decree was liable to the famous 'indictment for illegal proceedings', which, if upheld by the courts, quashed the decree, and also, if brought within a year, exposed the mover to heavy penalties. In the fifth century additions to the law were prepared by special legislative commissions, and then submitted to the council and assembly,[50] but there seems to have been no constitutional means of altering the existing law.[51]   After 403 an elaborate procedure was introduced for revising the law, which took the matter out of the hands of the assembly. Every year the assembly passed the laws under review, and voted on them, section by section, whether they should stand or be revised. If a revision of any section was voted, any citizen was entitled to propound alternative laws, which were given due publicity, and a court of 501 or 1,001 legislators was empanelled. The issue between the old and the proposed laws was then argued judicially (counsel for the old laws being appointed by the assembly), and the legislators, acting as a jury under oath, gave their verdict.[52]

Such was the Athenian theory on legislation. How far it was observed in practice is disputable. Both Demosthenes and Aeschines,[53] when bringing indictments for illegal proceedings, inveigh against the unscrupulous politicians (their opponents) who flout the law, and Demosthenes alleges that as a result 'there are so many contradictory laws that you have for a long while past been electing commissions to resolve the conflict, and none the less the problem can have no end. Laws are no different from decrees, and the laws, according to which decrees ought to be indicted, are more recent than the decrees themselves.' These strictures may be taken with a grain of salt. Politicians no doubt often tried to by-pass the rather cumbrous procedure for legislation—Demosthenes did so himself through Apollodorus over the allocation of the theoric fund.[54] But the indictment for illegal proceedings was a favourite political weapon, often invoked, as by Aeschines against Demosthenes on the famous issue of the Crown, on very technical grounds. And Aristophon's boast that he had been indicted (unsuccessfully) seventy-five times.[55] if it proves that some politicians often sailed near the wind, also proves that there were many jealous watchdogs of the constitution; Demosthenes' attempt to evade the law was, incidentally, foiled and Apollodorus suffered.[56]

On the other aspect of the rule of law Athenian democrats held exactly the opposite view to Aristotle's. 'Tyrannies and oligarchies', according to Aeschines,[57] 'are governed by the ways of their governments, democratic cities by the established laws.' 'No one, I think, would assert', says Demosthenes,[58] 'that there is any more important cause for the blessings which the city enjoys and for its being democratic and free, than the laws.' In another passage[59] Demosthenes contrasts law and oligarchy, declaring that in the latter any member of the government can revoke existing rules and make arbitrary enactments about the future, whereas the laws lay down what must be done for the future and are passed by persuasion in the interests of all. To Lycurgus[60] of 'the three most important factors which maintain and preserve democracy', the first is the law. Hypereides[61] declares it all-important 'that in a democracy the laws shall be sovereign'.

Both sides were naturally thinking of the worst specimens of the opposite party. Athenian democrats inevitably called to mind the arbitrary excesses of their own Four Hundred and Thirty when they spoke of oligarchies, and oligarchs could no doubt cite democracies whose acts were as brutal and illegal. On the whole the Athenian democracy seems to have lived up to its principles. Xenophon[62] has given us a vivid picture of one occasion when the assembly in a hysterical mood rode roughshod over its own rules of procedure and condemned the generals in command at Arginusae to death by one summary vote. But the emphasis given to this incident suggests that it was very exceptional. And Xenophon,[63] no favourable witness to the democracy, also testifies that after the restoration of the democracy in 403 the people religiously observed the amnesty agreed with the supporters of the Thirty. When one reads Xenophon's and Aristotle's record of the doings of the Thirty, one cannot but be amazed at the steadfast forbearance of the Athenian people.

The final and principal charge brought by the philosophers against democracy was that it meant the rule of the poor majority over the rich minority in their own interest. This is the main thesis of the 'Old Oligarch', whose treatise on the Athenian constitution takes the form of an ironical appreciation of its efficiency in promoting the interests of 'the bad' (the poor) at the expense of 'the good' (the rich); he is equally cynical in assuming that 'the good', if they got the chance, would govern in their own interest to the detriment of 'the bad'.[64] Plato in the *Republic*[65] declares that 'democracy results when the poor defeat the others and kill or expel them and share the constitution and the offices equally with the rest'. Aristotle[66] is very insistent that democracy is directed to the advantage of the indigent, going so far as to say that if, *per impossibile*, there should be more rich than poor in a city, the rule of the poor minority should be called democracy, and that of the rich majority oligarchy.

This view was naturally not accepted by democrats. Their views are doubtless reflected in the speech put into the mouth of the Syracusan democrat Athenagoras by Thucydides:[67]

It will be said that democracy is neither wise nor fair, and that the possessors of property are best qualified to rule well. My opinion is first that the people is the name of the whole, and oligarchy of a part, and secondly that the rich are the best guardians of property, the wise the best councillors, and the masses can best hear and judge, and that all these elements alike, jointly and severally, have an equal share in democracy.

It is more difficult to answer the question whether the Athenian democracy did or did not in fact exploit the rich for the benefit of the poor. In the distribution of political power and influence the rich seem to have fared well. In the minor offices and on the council and in the juries the poor no doubt predominated, though even here it would seem that by the fourth century the well-to-do were by no means crowded out. To the important military, diplomatic and financial offices men of birth and wealth were generally elected.[68] The orators, who, normally holding no office, guided policy by their speeches in the assembly were also mostly well-to-do, and many of them of good family.[69] It was comparatively rarely that a self-made man like Phrynichus or Aeschines achieved political influence. A rich man or an aristocrat certainly did not find that his political career was prejudiced by his wealth or birth, while poor and humbly born politicians had to face a good deal of abuse from comedians and orators.

Isocrates complains bitterly of the fiscal exploitation of the rich. In the *de Pace*[70] he rolls out a list of taxes and charges 'which cause so much vexation that property owners lead a harder life than utter paupers', and in the *Antidosis* he declares: 'when I was a boy it was thought to be such a secure and grand thing to be rich that practically everyone pretended to possess a larger property than he actually did, in his desire to acquire this reputation. But now one has to prepare a defence to prove that one is not rich, as if it were a great crime.'[71] From the meagre figures which we possess it is difficult to check these allegations. Normal peacetime expenditure (including the pay of citizens for political services) was defrayed from a variety of indirect taxes, a tax on resident aliens, royalties from the silver mines, rents of public and sacred land, court fees and fines and confiscations imposed by the courts. Certain religious festivals were financed by the system of liturgies, whereby rich men were nominated to produce plays, train teams of athletes and the like. In time of war it was often necessary to raise a property tax, which fell, it would seem, on about 6,000 persons, or a third to a quarter of the citizen body. In war time also the richest of the citizens were nominated as trierarchs, in which capacity they had to maintain a trireme in seaworthy condition for a year.

The war tax, of which great complaints were made, averaged over twenty years in the fourth century at a rate equivalent to a 5d. or 6d. in the pound income tax. We need not therefore take the laments of Isocrates and his like very seriously. The tax seems in fact to have been too widely spread, and did cause hardship to the poorest of those liable. It was, as appears from Demosthenes' speeches, very difficult to get the assembly, a substantial proportion of whom were taxpayers, to vote a levy, and hence wars were always inadequately financed.[72] Liturgies are much more difficult to calculate, as it depended greatly on the individual concerned how often he undertook them and how much he spent on each. It was useful political advertisement, almost a form of canvassing, to put up good shows,[73] and rich men were often very willing to acquire popularity by serving frequently and spending lavishly on gorgeous costumes and high salaries to stars. An evidently very rich man for whom Lysias[74] wrote a speech boasts that he undertook eleven liturgies in six years, spending in all nearly 3½ talents—a middle-class fortune. But, as he remarks, he need not have spent on them a quarter of this sum if he had confined himself to the strict requirements of the law; nor need he have performed more than a maximum of four liturgies.[75] At the other extreme another very rich man, Meidias, had, according to Demosthenes,[76] performed only one liturgy at the age of nearly fifty, and Dicaeogenes, another wealthy man, only undertook two minor ones in ten years.[77] The trierarchy was a heavier burden than the ordinary liturgies, costing from 40 to 60 minae (⅔ to 1 talent) a year,[78] and as it might fall on fortunes of 5 talents,[79] the temporary strain on a poor trierarch's resources would be severe. For this reason the burden was usually from the end of the fifth century shared between two holders,[80] and from 357 the 1,200 persons liable to trierarchic service were divided into twenty groups, whose members shared the expense:[81] thus, if a fleet of 100 ships were commissioned, twelve men would share the charge for each trierarchy. Here again the incidence of the burden varied greatly. The same man who performed eleven liturgies served seven years as trierarch during the Ionian war, spending 6 talents,[82] and a certain Aristophanes (with his father) served three trierarchies in four or five years in the Corinthian War, spending 80 minae in all.[83] Isocrates, on the other hand, who complains so bitterly of the oppression of the rich, and had made a large fortune by his rhetorical teaching, could at the age of 80 boast of only three trierarchies (including those performed by his son).[84] But it would be unfair to the Athenian upper classes to take the parsimonious orator as typical. As a public-spirited citizen we may instance the father of one of Lysias' clients, who in a career of fifty years (which included the Peloponnesian and Corinthian wars) was trierarch seven times. His son proudly displayed to the jury his father's accounts, which showed that he had altogether disbursed on trierarchies, liturgies and war tax 9 talents 20 minae,[85] an average of over 11 minae per annum. His fortune is not stated, but he certainly was a very rich man, since he entered chariots for the Isthmia and Nemea,[86] and is likely to have possessed substantially more than 15 talents, which Demosthenes implies would qualify a man to be called really rich.[87] If so, his contribution to the state would not have exceeded one-eighth of his income.

The taxation of the rich was very erratic, falling heavily in war years, and was badly distributed; before 357 all persons on the trierarchic register took their turn, though some were much richer than others, and after 357 all members of a group contributed equally.[88] This lack of system enabled some rich men to escape very lightly, and was on occasions oppressive to those with moderate fortunes. On the other hand, many rich men liked to make a splash, undertaking more trierarchies and liturgies than their legal quota, and thereby easing the burden of the others.

In general, it would seem that the average burden borne by the well-to-do in Athens was well within their means, though its erratic incidence might cause them temporary embarrassment.

The critics, however, allege that a more sinister method of soaking the rich than taxation was in vogue at Athens—that of condemning them on trumped-up charges and confiscating their property.[89] There is reason to believe that this abuse of the law courts did sometimes occur, but it is very difficult to say whether it was common.

Some general considerations need to be clarified. Athens, like all ancient States, relied for the enforcement of the law on the services of informers, and was obliged to reward them for convictions. Professional informers seem to have been a pest at Athens; but so they were everywhere—one has only to think of the reputation of *delatores* in imperial Rome. The State did not encourage frivolous accusations, subjecting to severe penalties an informer who failed to win a fifth of the jury's votes, or who abandoned a prosecution which he had instituted. Nor does it appear that informers were popular with juries. Defendants try to insinuate that their prosecutors are informers, and prosecutors, in their anxiety to prove they are not informers, sometimes go so far as to claim to be personal enemies, or even hereditary enemies, of the accused. Nevertheless, informers seem to have plied a busy trade, principally in blackmailing rich men who had guilty consciences or disliked facing the ordeal of public trial. This state of affairs naturally caused the propertied classes much anxiety, and perhaps caused them to exaggerate the real scope of the evil.[90]

Secondly, Athens, like all ancient States, lived from hand to mouth, and reckoned on the penalties inflicted by the courts as a regular source of income. It was therefore a temptation to jurors to vote in the interests of the treasury when money was short, and an informer dangled before their eyes a fat estate whose owner, he alleged, had been guilty of some serious offence. In this respect also Athens was not unique; Roman emperors short of money are alleged to have encouraged *delatores* and made good the finances by confiscation. Nor need one go so far afield as the Roman empire for a parallel. The Athenian oligarchs in the Thirty filled their treasury by condemning a number of innocuous but wealthy citizens and metics to death and seizing their property.[91] This situation also made the propertied classes nervous, and probably made them exaggerate the evil. There is no reason to believe that all large estates confiscated were confiscated because they were large. Rich Athenians were quite capable of cheating the treasury or betraying the interests of the State; and it is, for instance, very unlikely that a statesman of such severe probity as Lycurgus would have secured the confiscation of the huge estate—160 talents—of Diphilus, unless he had been guilty of a serious breach of the mining laws.[92]

There are three passages in Lysias[93] which allude to the abuse. In a speech written in 399 a litigant states that 'the council for the time being, when it has enough money for the administration, behaves correctly, but when it gets into difficulties it is obliged to receive impeachments and confiscate the property of the citizens and listen to the worst of the politicians'. In another speech, written about ten years later, another litigant says to the jury: 'You must remember that you have often heard them (his opponents) saying, when they wanted to ruin someone unjustly, that, if you would not condemn the people they tell you to condemn, your pay will fail.' And in a third speech, delivered in 387, a man accused of detaining the confiscated estate of a relative complains: 'My defence is difficult in view of the opinion some hold about Nicophemus' estate, and the present shortage of money in the city, my case being against the treasury.' These are serious allegations, and indicate an unhealthy state of affairs. But it is to be noted that they all occur in the period following the fall of Athens, when the State was almost bankrupt, and when, despite the amnesty, feeling against the rich, many of whom had backed the Thirty, was very bitter among the mass of the citizens. I have not detected any other similar suggestion in all the later speeches, forensic or political, of the orators, except one sentence

in the Fourth Philippic of Demosthenes,[94] when, after appealing
to the rich not to grudge to the poor their theoric payments, he
turns to the poor, and says: 'But where does the difficulty arise?
What is the trouble? It is when they see some people transferring
to private fortunes the practice established for public moneys,
and a speaker is great in your eyes at the moment, and immortal
as far as security goes—but the secret vote is different from the
open applause. This breeds distrust and anger.' This very guarded
passage seems to mean that the rich suspected that the poor
wished to increase their payments from public funds by confiscating private property, and that rich men who were applauded in
the assembly were condemned by the secret ballot of the juries.
Hypereides,[95] a few years later, takes pride in the disinterested
justice of Athenian juries:

There is no people or king or nation in the world more magnanimous than
the people of Athens. It does not abandon to their fate those of the citizens,
whether individuals or classes, who are falsely accused, but goes to their rescue.
In the first place when Teisis denounced the estate of Euthycrates, which was
worth more than sixty talents, as being public property, and after that again
promised to denounce the estate of Philip and Nausicles, alleging that they
acquired their wealth from unregistered mines, the jury, so far from welcoming
such a speech or coveting other men's goods, promptly disfranchised the false
accuser, not giving him a fifth of the votes. And again does not the recent
action of the jurors last month deserve great praise? When Lysander denounced
the mine of Epicrates as having been sunk within the boundaries—the mine
he had been working for three years and pretty well all the richest men in the
city were his partners—and Lysander promised to bring in 300 talents for the
city—that is what he said they had got out of the mine—nevertheless the jury
paid no attention to the accuser's promise but looked only to justice and
declared the mine private.

Hypereides perhaps protests too much, but he does at least provide concrete instances when Athenian juries resisted very tempt-
ing baits.

If one may attempt to draw a general conclusion it would be
that informers were a nuisance to the rich at Athens, and that the
Athenian courts were sometimes tempted, especially in financial
crises, to increase the revenue by condemning rich defendants

on insufficient evidence. Neither of these abuses was, however, peculiar to a democratic régime.

These are the main criticisms brought by the philosophers against the Athenian democracy. Some are directed against abuses which democrats agreed to be such, the overriding of the law by the executive enactments of the assembly and the spoliation of the rich by the poor, but which they claimed to be alien to the principles of democracy. In these matters the Athenian people was certainly not beyond reproach, but on the whole the charges seem to have been exaggerated, and the Athenians were probably justified in claiming that arbitrary violence of this kind was more characteristic of oligarchic régimes than of their own.

Other criticisms are on points of principle and are based on an entirely different conception of the functions of the State and an entirely different estimate of human nature. The philosophers held that the State ought to mould and train the citizens in virtue, and assumed that the average man was naturally evil or at least foolish. Political power must therefore be given to a select group of wise good men, who would impose a good way of life on the rest by a rigid system of education and control. The Athenian democrats, on the other hand, took an optimistic view of human nature, and believed that every citizen should be allowed to live his own life in his own way, within the broad limits laid down by the law, and that all citizens could be trusted to take their part in the government of the city, whether by voting and speaking in the assembly, judging in the juries, carrying on the routine administration as magistrates, or selecting the men to hold high political office. On one point the Athenians were distrustful of human nature, on its ability to resist the temptations of irresponsible power;[96] hence their insistence on brief terms of office, regular review of the conduct of magistrates in office, and above all a searching scrutiny of the record of magistrates on completing their term. The philosophers are strangely blind to this danger, and are content to rely on the virtue of their usually hereditary or co-optative oligarchies of wise men.

The ideals of the Athenian democracy are perhaps best summed up in a rather florid passage of the Funeral Oration attributed to Lysias.[97] Our ancestors, he says,

were the first and only men of that time who cast out arbitrary power and established democracy, holding that the freedom of all was the greatest concord, and sharing with one another their hopes and perils they governed themselves with free hearts, honouring the good and chastising the bad by law. They held it bestial to constrain one another by force, and the part of men to define justice by law, and to persuade by reason, and serve both by action, having law as their king and reason as their teacher.

Thucydides has very little to say on the internal government of Athens; it is with the foreign and imperial policy of the democracy that he is concerned. Here he makes only one explicit charge, that of incompetence. Under Pericles, when the régime was 'nominally a democracy but really government by the first citizen', Athens pursued a considered and consistent policy of husbanding her resources and undertaking no new commitments. By this policy she could, in Thucydides' opinion, have won the war. But when Pericles' unique authority was removed, 'his successors, being more on a level with one another and each struggling to gain the ascendancy, tended to surrender political decisions to the pleasure of the people'. The greatest mistake, he goes on, was the Sicilian expedition, not so much because it was 'an error of judgement in relation to its objective', but because 'those who sent it out did not give proper support to the expedition in their subsequent decisions, but in the course of their private cabals about the leadership of the people were slack in their conduct of the war and at home began to fall into intestine disorders'.[98]

It would be a long task to discuss whether Athens could have won the war on the purely defensive strategy which Thucydides attributes to Pericles, and whether the Sicilian expedition had a reasonable prospect of success. It may, however, be noted in passing that Thucydides' narrative does not bear out his charge that the Athenian people gave inadequate support to the expedi-

tion. It is indisputable that it was a serious blunder to risk so large
a force on a distant expedition with an unconquered enemy at
their gates, and that the Athenian people showed lack of judgment in succumbing to Alcibiades' eloquence. But it is hardly
fair to condemn a whole régime for one blunder. Taking a
longer view it cannot be said that the Athenians conducted their
affairs unwisely. It took the Spartans and their Peloponnesian
allies thirty years to bring to a successful conclusion a war which
they had innocently hoped to win in two or three seasons, and
they only won it in the end by cynically bartering 'the freedom
of the Greeks', for which they were professedly fighting, to the
national enemy Persia in return for subsidies. In the whole course
of its history the Athenian democracy may be said to have been
the most successful State in Greece. With no especial advantages
except its silver mines it made itself the greatest city in the Greek
world for the fifty years between the Persian and Peloponnesian
wars, and after the great defeat in 404 rapidly rose again to be
one of the first-class powers, a position which it held till crushed
by Macedonia with the rest of Greece. Nor were strategic and
political blunders a peculiarity of democracies. It would be hard
to find in Athenian history any parallel to Sparta's ineptitude
after her great victory over Athens. Only political incompetence
of the highest order could have ranged in alliance against herself
her two most faithful allies, Corinth and Thebes, and her and
their two bitterest enemies, Argos and Athens. But to break
simultaneously with the Great King and launch a crusade into
Asia Minor shows utter irresponsibility. The results were disastrous to Sparta in the loss of her newly won maritime empire,
the revival of Athens as a great power, and the permanent hostility
of Thebes.

Thucydides' attitude is not difficult to understand. He was
clearly a profound admirer of Pericles. Equally clearly he was
strongly prejudiced against the type of statesman who succeeded him, notably Cleon.[99] It would be out of place here to
discuss Cleon's merits, though it is worth noting that later genera-

tions did not share Thucydides' low opinion of him; a wealthy Athenian in 350 B.C. is proud to claim that his mother's first husband had been Cleomedon, 'whose father Cleon, we are told, as general of your ancestors captured a large number of Spartans alive at Pylos and was the most distinguished man in the city';[100] but no reader can fail to note Thucydides' rancour against him. As a patriotic Athenian Thucydides was deeply distressed at his city's ruin. It was natural that in his bitterness he should be unfair to the politicians whom he hated and to the régime which had given them power.

Explicitly Thucydides blames the democracy only for its incompetent conduct of the war. Implicitly he accuses it of a cynical and brutal imperialism which, he suggests, was followed by a just retribution. This result is achieved in a variety of ways; by the choice of words in describing Athenian actions, by the selection and stressing of certain incidents in the narrative, and by the speeches put into the mouths of Athenian politicians. A good example of the first method is the language used by Thucydides to describe the Athenian reduction of Naxos, the first ally which attempted to secede—the city 'was enslaved contrary to established usage' (παρὰ τὸ καθεστηκὸς ἐδουλώθη).[101] We are not told what precisely was done to Naxos, which later appears as a normal subject city, paying a rather low tribute but with part of its territory occupied by an Athenian cleruchy. By analogy with similar cases we may infer that the Naxians had to surrender their fleet and pay tribute instead of contributing ships to the federal fleet; that the oligarchic government, which had proved disloyal to the league, was replaced by a democracy; and that the estates of the oligarchs were confiscated, later to be partitioned among Athenian settlers. The word 'enslave' is rather a sinister word to describe this, and the vague adverbial phrase suggests, without defining, moral obliquity.[102]

The chief example of the second method is the immense stress laid on the mass execution of the Melians by means of the long debate between the Athenians and their victims, which is immediately followed by the rash decision of the assembly to undertake the Sicilian expedition, the description of the proud armada, and the long-drawn-out agony of its utter destruction. Every reader of Thucydides is left with the impression that Athens had sinned greatly, and that retribution fell upon her; and there can be no doubt that is what Thucydides felt and wished his readers to feel.

The chief speech in which Thucydides points his moral is the famous Melian dialogue,[103] where the Athenian delegates brush aside all moral considerations and openly propound the doctrine that might is right. In a similar spirit Cleon in the debate on the fate of the Mitylenaeans declares that the empire is a tyranny which must be maintained by terror,[104] and his opponent Diodotus urges clemency purely on grounds of expediency. Other speeches of importance are that of Pericles after the second invasion of Attica, when he too proclaims the empire a tyranny,[105] and the defence of the empire put up by an Athenian delegate at Sparta before the opening of the war and again at Camarina during the Sicilian expedition. In both of these the empire is frankly admitted to rest on force alone. The first speaker claims that Athens may be excused for clinging to it on the grounds of prestige, profit and fear (of what she would suffer from her subjects if she relaxed her grip), and urges in mitigation of the offence that Athens used her power with moderation.[106] The second speaker endeavours to allay Sicilian misgivings by pointing out that while it was in Athens' interest to oppress the allies at home, in Sicily she would have no motive for doing so.[107]

The speeches in Thucydides are a difficult problem. He himself says that it was 'difficult for me, when I myself heard them, and for my informants in other cases, to remember exactly what was said; I have made the various characters speak as I thought they would have spoken most appropriately about the situations which arose, keeping as closely as possible to the general tenor of what was actually said'.[108] It is possible to interpret these words in many different ways, and to evaluate the several speeches very

variously according to whether Thucydides is likely to have been
present himself or to have had trustworthy informants. It is
virtually impossible that he can have had any information on the
Melian debate, which was held behind closed doors between the
Athenian commissioners and the Melian government, who were
all subsequently executed, and it must be regarded as a free composition. Thucydides was not present at Sparta or at Camarina.
On the other hand, he probably listened to Pericles and to the
Mitylenaean debate.

If these speeches are intended to reproduce the actual tenor of
Athenian public utterances, it must be admitted that the Athenians of the fifth century not only were a very remarkable, if
not unique, people in openly admitting that their policy was
guided purely by selfish considerations and they had no regard
for political morality, but also that they underwent a complete
transformation in the fourth century, when we possess genuine
speeches. In these, the Funeral Speech attributed to Lysias and
the *Panegyricus* and *Panathenaicus* of Isocrates, the speakers dilate
not only on the glories of their former empire, but on its high
purposes. By it Athens had kept Greece free from Persian rule,
and had so humbled the Great King that he had formally re-
nounced his right to enter the Aegean. Athens had given her
allies not only prosperity, but freedom, everywhere liberating
them from the yoke of tyrannies and oligarchies and bestowing
upon them the blessings of democracy, and they had fought by
her side, not for her supremacy but for their own freedom.[109]
The same theme is parodied by Plato in the *Menexenus*—'we
fought the Spartans at Tanagra for the freedom of the Boeotians',
'we won many victories in Sicily for the freedom of the Leontines'.[110] And in the political orations of Demosthenes in the
latter part of the century an idealistic note is always struck—
Athenians should everywhere champion democracy, Athens
should be the leader of free Greece against the tyranny of Macedon.

It is difficult to resist the conclusion that Thucydides, in order to point his moral, put into the mouths of Athenian spokesmen what he considered to be their real sentiments, stripped of rhetorical claptrap, and that what we have in the speeches is in effect Thucydides' own opinion of the empire. His view was that Athens was universally hated by her allies or subjects, who were held down by fear or force only, and were eager to revolt on every possible opportunity—this thesis he twice states in his own person apart from the speeches[111]—and that Athens was wrong in 'enslaving' them, by her refusal to allow them to secede from the league and by her interference in their internal government. Furthermore, that the Athenians, to enforce their tyranny (as with Mitylene) or to enlarge it (as with Melos) committed or very nearly committed acts of the grossest brutality. Let us examine the validity of Thucydides' view.

His main thesis can be proved from his own narrative to be grossly oversimplified, and he himself gives the key to the truth in the statement which he attributes to Diodotus in the Mitylenaean debate. 'At present the people in all the cities is friendly to you, and either does not join in revolt with the few, or if it is compelled to do so, is immediately hostile to the rebels, and you go to war with the majority of the opposing city on your side.'[112] This analysis is borne out by almost every case where the story of a revolt is told in any detail. At Mitylene the ruling oligarchy (presumably the thousand-odd persons who were ultimately executed as being most responsible for the revolt) seceded; the people, as soon as the Spartan commandant issued arms to them, mutinied, and the city promptly surrendered.[113] Brasidas in Thrace had to lecture the Acanthians on their duty to accept the freedom which he offered them, and to clinch the argument by a threat to destroy their vintage.[114] At Torone and Mende also small cliques of conspirators admitted Brasidas, and at the latter town the people rallied to the Athenians as soon as a relieving force arrived, and were entrusted by Nicias with the punishment of their own traitors.[115] At Chios, even after the Sicilian disaster, the oligarchic government did not dare to break with

Athens for fear of the masses till a Spartan fleet arrived.[116] At Rhodes, shortly afterwards, certain prominent persons intrigued with the Spartans, and the arrival of a powerful fleet 'terrified the majority, who were unaware of what was going on'.[117] The people of Samos, having purged their oligarchs in successive revolutions, remained faithful to Athens to the bitter end.[118] There were some cities where hostility to Athens was more widespread, but in general the malcontents seem to have been limited to oligarchic groups. Thucydides' estimate of public opinion was no doubt based on his contacts with men of this type, whom he would have met before his exile as visitors to Athens and during his exile intriguing with the Spartans. His own meticulously fair and accurate narrative, however, proves that his estimate was seriously at fault.

Even if this be so, however, does it remain true that, according to the accepted canons of Greek political morality, Athens acted wrongfully in refusing to allow her allies to secede, and in interfering with their internal government? All Greeks, of course, paid lip service to the principle of autonomy, but in practice powerful States did not allow it to incommode them, and public opinion did not condemn them. To judge Athens one may compare her conduct with that of the other leading State of Greece, Sparta, whose boast that her allies were autonomous is generally admitted in our sources.

When Tegea broke with Sparta and formed an alliance with Argos in about 465 the Spartans invaded her territory and defeated her at the battle of Tegea. When shortly afterwards all the Arcadian cities except Mantinea revolted, Sparta marched against them and defeated them at Dipaea.[119] When after the Peace of Nicias Mantinea and Elis seceded from the league and Tegea began to waver, Sparta again marched and won the battle of Mantinea; next year Mantinea returned to her allegiance.[120] Elis did not participate in the battle of Mantinea and was left alone for some years. But when Sparta's hands were free after the fall of Athens, Elis was subdued and brought to obedience again.[121] Sparta, in fact, did not allow her allies to secede,[122] and no one blamed her for reducing them to obedience if they tried to do so.

When Sparta delivered her ultimatum to Athens, 'the Spartans wish the peace to continue, and this would be so if you leave the Greeks autonomous', Pericles replied that they would do so 'when the Spartans also restore to their cities the right to govern themselves not in Spartan interests, but as they themselves severally wish'.[123] In fact, both Athens and Sparta supported in their allied cities governments favourable to themselves, Athens normally favouring democracies and Sparta oligarchies. Neither usually intervened arbitrarily, but when opportunity offered—when there was a conflict in an allied city and the defeated party appealed to the leading city, or when a hostile government had revolted and been subdued—they took advantage of it.[124] There were a few democracies among Sparta's allies—Elis and Mantinea, for instance—and a few oligarchies among Athens, Mitylene, Chios and Samos. It is noticeable that all these cities had been consistently loyal, and had thus given their suzerains no opportunity for intervention.

Thucydides also implies that the Athenians violated the rights of the allies by suppressing the federal congress of the Delian League. 'At first', he writes, 'the allies were independent under their leadership and determined policy as the result of federal congresses.'[125] By contrast with Athens Pericles emphasises the divided councils of the Peloponnesians, who all have an equal vote.[126] From the speech of the Mitylenaeans at the Olympia of 428, however, it would appear that as recently as 440 a Delian Congress had been held to decide what was to be done about Samos, and that the Mitylenaeans had voted for war; allusion is also made to the equal voting power of cities and to the large number of cities voting.[127] It would seem in fact that the constitution of the Delian League was exactly modelled on that of the Peloponnesian, where every city, great or small, had one vote,[128] and that the constitution was formally observed as late as 440 B.C.

No Delian Congress is reported by Thucydides before the Peloponnesian war, and doubtless none was held; for no declaration of war was required from the League, since Athens was attacked by the Peloponnesians in violation of the Thirty Years' Peace.[129]

De facto the position of Athens and Sparta in their respective leagues was very different. Sparta had no overwhelming military predominance over her allies and had therefore to take some account of their sentiments and interests, particularly as there was in Corinth a potential leader of the opposition, which could, and sometimes did, sway the majority of the congress against her.[130] Athens from the beginning enjoyed naval predominance because many of the allies subscribed not ships but money, which in effect subsidised the Athenian fleet, and as more and more allies either commuted to money for their own convenience, or were compelled to do so after revolt, Athenian ascendancy became overwhelming. The Delian Congress therefore tended to ratify Athenian decisions automatically, particularly as the naval allies did not show the independent spirit of Corinth; even as late as 440 B.C., if Chios and the Lesbian cities had stood up for Samos, they could, with about 200 ships between them, have given Athens pause.[131]

Athens in this position undoubtedly kept a tighter rein on her allies, notably in concentrating criminal jurisdiction in her own hands and thus making sure that her friends in the allied cities were protected and her enemies suffered.[132] She also exploited her allies more openly, especially in using a part of the federal reserve fund to rebuild her own temples and in apportioning to her own citizens land forfeited by rebellious allied communities or individuals. Sparta had no temptation or opportunity to do the like, but she used her allies for her own purposes, above all to protect her against Helot revolts.[133] Both Sparta and Athens, despite their rival protestations that they stood for the autonomy of the Hellenes or liberty and democracy, in fact used their leagues to secure their own political supremacy. The Peloponnesian

League was on the whole satisfactory to the oligarchic governments of its member States, the Delian to the people in the allied cities.

On the score of brutality no one will wish to defend the decision —happily reversed the next day—to massacre the whole adult population of Mitylene, nor the execution of the Melians, or of the Scionaeans (which Thucydides dismisses without comment). It must, however, be said that in neither of the two cases which he treats in detail is Thucydides quite fair. In the speeches which he reports he represents the repeal of the Mitylenaean decision as a prudential measure only; whereas he records that the second debate was held because 'on the next day they immediately had a change of heart and reflected that this decision, to destroy a whole city instead of the guilty parties, was a great barbarity'.[134] In the Melian dialogue Thucydides implies that Melos was an unoffending neutral, which Athens found it convenient to subdue. In point of fact Melos had been a non-belligerent ally of Sparta since the beginning of the war, subscribing to her war fund and sheltering her fleet in 427,[135] and Athens had, not unnaturally, been at war with the Melians since 426.[136]

Here also Athens was not exceptional, nor did she lead the way. The Spartans set the example by the even more gratuitous massacre of the Plataeans. The Mitylenaeans and Scionaeans were at least in Athenian eyes traitors, allies who had broken their oaths, and the Melians had assisted their enemies. The Plataeans had been guilty of defending their own city when treacherously attacked by Thebes in time of peace. The only question which the Spartan judges put to them was 'whether they had done any good to the Spartans and their allies during the war'; they were in fact condemned simply for being on the other side.[137]

The Athenians, in fact, can only be condemned, if they are judged by much more lofty standards than were normally applied to international relations. Why did Thucydides take so uncharitable a view of his native city? His attitude was partly due to a misconception of public feeling natural to a man of his class, particularly when he had for many years lived in exile in oligarchic circles. He appears to have really believed that the Athenians were hated by their allies, whereas the Peloponnesian League was a free association of cities. But his attitude was also probably due to a deep-seated and perhaps unconscious desire to find a moral justification for the fall of Athens. It was not enough to say that it was due to the folly of the democratic politicians whom he so much disliked. It must have been deserved. Athens had suffered grievously; this could not have been so if she had not sinned greatly.

The opinions of Thucydides, Plato and Aristotle have naturally carried great weight, and so, curiously enough, have those of Isocrates. In the absence of any coherent statement of the democratic case, most modern historians have rather uncritically accepted the oligarchic view of Athens, and condemned what Aristotle calls the 'extreme democracy'.[138] In this article I have endeavoured to reconstruct the theory of government in which democrats believed and to assess the merits and defects of the Athenian democracy in the conduct of home affairs and of foreign and imperial policy. My readers can judge whether the 'extreme democracy', in which the people was sovereign, and vulgar persons who worked with their hands enjoyed full political rights, including access to all offices, and owing to their greater numbers preponderated in the assembly, was indeed so pernicious a form of government as Athenian philosophers and historians represent.

IV

THE SOCIAL STRUCTURE OF ATHENS IN THE FOURTH CENTURY B.C.

The Social Structure of Athens in the Fourth Century B.C.

T HE political history of Athens and its literature, philosophy and art have not unnaturally received far more attention than its economic life. The achievements of the Athenian people in the former spheres were outstanding, and we possess an abundance of material for their study. In the economic field on the other hand the record of Athens is less striking, and the evidence is very scrappy and incomplete. Nevertheless, the subject perhaps deserves more intensive study than it has received. Inadequate though the evidence is for Athens it is far richer than for any other ancient city, and if the economic history of the ancient world is a feasible subject of study, it should start with the economic history of Athens. And for a full understanding of the achievements of the Athenian people in other spheres some knowledge of the material background is desirable if not essential. It adds something to our appreciation of Attic drama to know how the audience for which it was written lived, even more to our appreciation of the Attic orators to know what kind of men attended the assembly and sat on the juries. To understand the political philosophy of Plato and Aristotle it is essential to know something of the society in which they lived. Above all it is impossible fully to understand and appreciate the great political achievement of Athens, the democracy, unless we know what kind of men were the citizens who debated and voted in the assembly and the council, administered the State as magistrates and decided legal and political issues as jurors in the popular courts. Ancient critics, Plato, Isocrates, and Aristotle, denounced the democracy as a tyranny of the poor over the rich. Modern critics have declared that the democracy was a fraud, and the citizens were a leisured minority living on the labour of slaves. It is of some moment to discover which, if either, of these views is true.

In what follows I have attempted a factual analysis of Athenian society in the fourth century B.C. I have tried to determine how many free persons, citizens or foreigners, lived in Attica; how many were rich, well-to-do or poor; what proportion lived on unearned incomes, or worked on the land, or were craftsmen or labourers; how many slaves of various kinds—domestic servants, farm labourers, miners or craftsmen—Athenians and foreigners of various classes owned. I have perforce confined myself to the fourth century, and for the most part to the middle and later decades of that century, because it is only for that period that we possess even the rudimentary statistical information necessary for such an analysis, and also, thanks mainly to the private speeches of the orators, a relative abundance of intimate detail on some aspects of the Athenian economy.

The first question we have to ask is how many Athenian citizens there were: by this I mean how many adult males (from 20 upwards), and in all that follows I shall mean (unless I specify otherwise) adult males, because we do not know how many women and children there were. Demetrius of Phalerum (317-307 B.C.) took a census, in which 21,000 were counted.[1] An orator contemporary with Demosthenes says rather casually 20,000.[2] And when at the bidding of Antipater in 322 the constitution was altered, so that only owners of property assessed at 20 minae or more remained citizens, 9,000 were registered as citizens, and according to the text of Plutarch, 12,000 were disfranchised, according to that of Diodorus, 22,000. The first figure, which yields a grand total of 21,000, seems to me more likely.[3]

Besides citizens there were resident aliens or metics: we have only one figure—Demetrius of Phalerum's census gave 10,000. There were, of course, also slaves owned by citizens and metics. For these we have two very extraordinary figures. According to Athenaeus (our sole source) 400,000 were counted at the census of Demetrius of Phalerum, that is an average of thirteen per head for every citizen or metic, rich or poor. The Lexicon of Suidas[4] cites half a sentence from Hypereides, 'more than 150,000 from the silver mines and over the rest of the country', which probably comes from the speech which Hypereides delivered in defence of his proposal to free the slaves after Chaeronea. This yields an average of five slaves per free man. I would not discuss these fantastic figures, if some scholars did not still take them seriously. The best test is the amount of wheat the population of Athens consumed, because we know more or less how much was consumed, and how much the normal person ate, and even slaves had to eat.

An Athenian inscription, recording the first-fruits offered to Demeter in 329 B.C., shows, on the likely hypothesis that the first-fruits were 1/600 of barley and 1/1200 of wheat, that in that year the crop of Attica was 28,500 medimni of wheat and 340,350 medimni of barley.[5] It may have been a bad year; we have no means of telling. I have no doubt that Athenian farmers all under-estimated their crops; so that the real crop was considerably larger. On the other hand we must deduct a proportion of the crop—about a sixth—for seed corn. The wheat was all used for human consumption, barley was not much eaten, and was reckoned at half the nutritive value;[6] much if not most of the barley must have been fed to animals.[7] However, these figures do not matter much, as they were chicken-feed in comparison with imports.

On these Demosthenes gives some apparently reliable figures in the Leptines, though he presents them in a rather curious way.[8] He first says that the wheat imported from the Pontus was about half the total imports; I do not know how he could have known this, and I do not think he did. He then says that the annual imports from the Pontus were about 400,000 medimni, and that this could be verified from the records by the sitophylakes, the magistrates charged with regulating the price of corn on the

Athenian market. The sitophylakes are likely to have kept a record of the total imports of wheat, but it would seem to be unnecessary and difficult for them to have kept a record of the country of origin of each cargo. I infer that Demosthenes looked up the figure of the imports, and found it to be 800,000 medimni, and on the quite unverified assertion that half came from the Pontus, told the jury that 400,000 came from the Pontus—which was what he wanted to prove. A total annual import of 800,000 medimni seems to be a genuine figure, in which case the total available for consumption was, say, 830,000 medimni of wheat (allowing for a considerable underestimate of the home crop in the Eleusis inscription), and such home-grown barley as was not fed to animals.

Now a man was generally reckoned to eat $7\frac{1}{2}$ and a woman or child about 5 medimni p.a.[9] Thirty-one thousand adult male citizens and metics would at this rate have eaten 232,000 medimni p.a. We do not, as I have said, know the average size of an Athenian family, but certain vital statistics which I shall come to later suggest that the population had a high birth-rate and a high death-rate, and that children would be, by modern British standards, a large element in the population. If therefore we assume that to every man there were three women and children (as in modern England) we shall be underestimating. Ninety-three thousand women and children (at three each to 31,000 adult males) each eating 5 medimni of wheat a year would consume 465,000 medimni p.a. The free population ought thus to have consumed a minimum of about 700,000 medimni p.a. out of a total of 830,000.

There was therefore a maximum of 130,000 medimni of wheat, plus an unknown quantity of barley, to feed slaves. We do not know how many of the slaves were women—most domestic servants were—and how many men—miners, agricultural labourers, craftsmen. Assuming the proportion was 50:50, and the average consumption of wheat by a slave therefore about 6 medimni, the slave population, male and female, was at a maximum about 20,000 as against approximately 62,000 free adults, male and female, or 124,000 free persons, including children.

All these figures have a very large margin of error, but are, I believe, of the right order of magnitude. They are at any rate of the same order of magnitude as two reputable figures that we possess for the slave population of Athens. Thucydides says that in the Decelean war more than 20,000 slaves, mainly skilled men, escaped;[10] but in 413 Athens was a much richer place than in the fourth century, and the free population much larger. Xenophon in his *Vectigalia* states that, if fully exploited, the Laurium mines could have provided employment for more than 10,000 slaves, and in confirmation of this statement declares that those, if any, who remembered what the slave tax used to bring in before the Decelean war (sixty years ago) would bear him out.[11] He clearly implies that in his own day the number of miners was very much smaller.

To return to the citizens: we are informed, as I have said before, that in 322 there were 12,000 citizens who owned less than 20 minae or 2,000 drachmae. There is reason to believe that these citizens were the Solonian class of thetes, who were not liable to military service as hoplites, but had to serve when occasion demanded as rowers in the fleet.[12] There is only one check on this figure of 12,000, that in 351 B.C. the assembly, presumably guided by the generals, resolved to commission forty triremes, to man which 8,000 men would be required, and for this purpose resolved to call up the age classes from 20 to 45.[13] Allowing for the probable age distribution of the population, to which I shall allude later, this would leave a fair margin.

Twenty minae is difficult to express in modern terms. According to the one contemporary figure we possess for the price of land, it would correspond to 5-6 acres of land, perhaps a holding of 5 acres with house and stock.[14] The 12,000 thetes owned less than this, but there is one fact which suggests that a large number of citizens owned land in minimal quantities. After the restoration of the democracy in 403 it was proposed that only Athenians holding land should be citizens, and fragments of a speech against this proposal survive. Dionysius of Halicarnassus, who had read the whole speech, says that the orator asserted that 5,000 persons would have been disfranchised under the proposal:[15] and he had every reason to overestimate the number. Conditions had no doubt changed since 403, but I know of no evidence which would disprove that about half the 12,000 thetes were landowners on a very small scale. This would be the natural result of the Athenian law of inheritance, whereby sons inherited equally, so that peasant holdings were more and more subdivided. Brothers often held their deceased father's holding in common. Many Athenian thetes may have earned money seasonally at Athens, and spent part of the year on the family farm.[16]

But some 5,000 Athenians owned no vestige of land. Some of them may have been quite comfortably off. Twenty minae was, according to Demosthenes, the equivalent of about six or seven skilled industrial slaves.[17] At the upper limit of the thetic class a man might own a house, incorporating a workshop, and say five skilled slaves. Below him were craftsmen who owned four, three, two or one slave, or who worked alone assisted by their children. At the bottom of the scale were, as today, casual labourers ($\mu\iota\sigma\theta\omega\tau o\iota$), who in the latter part of the fourth century, as the Eleusis accounts show, could earn 1½ drachmae a day when in work.[18]

Did many thetes live on state pay? There was the council of 500, on which a citizen could serve two years in his lifetime, receiving 5 obols (about half a labourer's rate) per day: on the evidence it was mostly persons of independent means who served on the council. There were about 350 magistrates, paid on slightly varying but similar scales; in these quite humble persons, poor hoplites and even thetes, seem to have served. Finally, there was a register of 6,000 persons, from whom the jurors were selected on court days. Those who actually served on a jury received 3 obols for the day's work.[19] Now this was what the Athenian people, humane but not overgenerous employers, allocated as their daily ration allowances to low-grade public slaves—labourers at the Eleusinium; these slaves received free lodging and clothes in addition.[20] In other words an Athenian juror could buy himself enough food to eat on the day that he sat in court, and no more. The out-of-work may have earned an odd day's keep in this way; but once again the tone of the speeches delivered to Athenian juries suggests that most of the jurors were men of some substance.[21] All Athenian citizens could, of course, earn 1 drachma by attending the assembly on thirty days in the year, and on ten more $1\frac{1}{2}$ drachmae (a labourer's daily wage).[22] They could also draw 2 obols as theoricon on probably about six public holidays in the year.[23]

My conclusion, which is not very surprising, but does not accord with some popular misconceptions, is that out of a total population of 21,000 citizens, about 12,000, say 60 per cent., earned their living by working on very small holdings of 5 acres downwards, or as skilled craftsmen or shopkeepers, with from five slave assistants downwards, or as casual labourers.

We may now turn to the 9,000 persons (say 40 per cent. of the population) who owned over 20 minae, and were liable, if between the ages of 20 and 60, to serve as hoplites (the 1,000 richest as cavalry). This figure of 9,000, I would remind you, is attested for the year 322. Curiously enough 'the Five Thousand' in 411 B.C., when interpreted as meaning those who provided their own suits of armour, turned out to be 9,000 in number.[24] It may be a coincidence that there were 9,000 hoplites in 411 and again in 322, but it looks as if the general distribution of wealth was fairly stable throughout the fourth century. The few figures we possess for armies put into the field by Athens at intervals throughout the fourth century do not disagree, that is they are comfortably under 9,000,[25] and in the Lamian war in 323 the figures recorded by Diodorus, which yield 7,850 for the 20 to 40 age groups,[26] are according to my calculations compatible with a grand total of 9,000 citizens of hoplite census of all ages, on the assumption—which we know from Xenophon to be true—that metics of the appropriate property qualification and age groups had to serve.[27]

This depends on the age distribution of the population, for which we have slight but sure evidence from the inscriptions. Three inscriptions show that round about 330 B.C. an ephebe class, i.e. the young men of hoplite census aged 18 or 19, numbered about 500.[28] Another inscription shows that in 325/4 B.C. the arbitrators, that is citizens of hoplite class aged 60, numbered exactly 103.[29] These are startling figures, if compared with the census records of modern England, but Mr. A. R. Burn has recently demonstrated that the vital statistics of Roman Africa and Roman Carthage and sundry other areas under the Principate were not analogous to modern English figures, but to those of

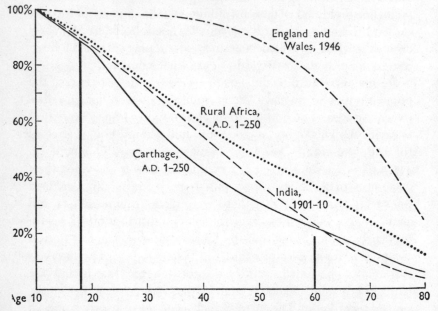

These graphs illustrate the percentages of males alive at the age of ten who reached successive ages up to eighty in Carthage (A.D. 1-250), rural Africa (A.D. 1-250), India (1901-10) and England and Wales (1946). The vertical lines show the proportion of ephebes (18) to arbitrators (60), in Athens in the fourth century B.C.

India at the beginning of this century.[30] There is no reason to believe that conditions in the fourth century B.C. in Athens and Attica were strikingly better than those in Carthage and Africa under the Principate, and in point of fact Mr. Burn's graphs, if applied to recorded Athenian figures, fit curiously well.[31] The main conclusion from his statistics, applied to Athenian figures, is that the Athenians suffered a uniformly high death rate from the age of 20 to 60 so that of 500 young men of 20 not many more than 100 survived to be 60 forty years later. Having reached about 60 a man was, it appears, so tough that he might easily live another ten or fifteen years. There are no ancient statistics of the child death rate, but it was probably at least as high as that of adults. The population would therefore have been very young, with a high percentage of children.

The line dividing hoplites from thetes was of course an arbitrary one, and there must have been many hoplites just over the line, who were relatively poor men. Demosthenes in the Meidias twice apologises for introducing to the jury a hoplite, Strato of Phalerum, who had served on all the expeditions for which his age group had been called up, and had finally been arbitrator— 'a poor man no doubt, but not a knave'.[32] Mantitheus, when his deme assembled for the muster, found that many of his poorer fellow hoplites could not even raise their journey money, and organised a subscription to provide them with 30 drachmae each.[33]

Here again we have some statistical data to guide us. The citizens liable to the eisphora, the war tax on property, were in 378-7 B.C. organised in 100 groups or symmories.[34] In 357-6 the symmory system was applied to the trierarchy, the duty of maintaining a warship for one year, and the 1,200 persons liable to serve were grouped in twenty symmories.[35] The business of the eisphora and of the trierarchy symmories was similar—to collect money from the members—and it is a plausible hypothesis that it was decided to group the 1,200 potential trierarchs in symmories of sixty persons each, because sixty had been found a convenient number in the eisphora symmories. If so, there will have been about 6,000 persons liable to the eisphora. There is evidence that 25 minae was a standard unit of assessment for the eisphora,[36] and it has been inferred that citizens who owned property assessed at less than this sum were exempt from eisphora. If so, an interesting conclusion emerges, that there were 3,000 citizens who owned between 20 and 25 minae—a farm with house and stock of from 5 to 6 acres.

We now come to the 6,000-odd citizens, assessed at 25 minae upwards, who paid eisphora. We have the evidence—for what it is worth—of Demosthenes that many of these were relatively poor. Castigating the harshness of Androtion and Timocrates when collecting the arrears of eisphora, he invokes the sympathy of the jury for their victims, 'farmers who pinch and scrape, but who owing to the cost of bringing up their children, and domestic expenses and other public demands, have fallen into arrears of eisphora'.[37] He depicts Androtion and Timocrates 'removing doors, and seizing blankets, and distraining on a servant girl, if any of them employed one'.[38] If Demosthenes is speaking the truth, some of the 6,000 eisphora payers could not even afford to buy a single slave girl to help in the house.

There is statistical evidence which corroborates Demosthenes. According to Polybius the total assessment of Attica was 5,750 talents, according to Philochorus and Demosthenes 6,000 talents: for convenience' sake I will adopt the latter figure. I have argued elsewhere what 'the total assessment' or 'the assessment of the country' means, and I shall only repeat my conclusion that theoretically it represented the gross total value of the property, in all forms, whether land, houses, personal effects, slaves, cash or investments, owned by the 6,000-odd persons who were assessed above 25 minae and paid eisphora.[39] Some economic historians have thought the figure unduly small, but it must, I think, be accepted for what it purports to be. It is likely to be an underestimate, for to judge by many allusions in the orators, it was the exception rather than the rule that an Athenian taxpayer declared the whole of his property. Land and houses were however difficult to conceal, and these were probably the main items. Slaves might be underestimated both in numbers and value. Cash and loans could be concealed altogether. But there were sycophants, and one of the reasons for the reign of terror which they are alleged to have exercised over the wealthy may well have been that most wealthy men knew that their eisphora assessments would not bear investigation.

Now, if 6,000 persons were assessed at 6,000 talents, their average property would be one talent. But, as we shall see, there were among the Three Hundred, who were responsible for the collection of the eisphora, men who owned upwards of 15 talents, and among the 1,200 on the trierarchic register quite a number who owned about 5 talents. It must follow that in the lower half or two-thirds of the 6,000 the average fortune must have been well below 1 talent; a large group must have owned between 25 and 30 minae ($\frac{1}{2}$ a talent) each, and these are probably the poor farmers whom Demosthenes describes.

Now we come to the Athenian upper class, which roughly corresponded with the 1,200 persons on the trierarchic register: there was no property qualification for trierarchic service, and the list was supposed to include the 1,200 richest Athenians. We know a great deal about many individuals in this class, because in their mutual litigation about inheritances, trierarchies, liturgies, dowries, etc., they could afford to employ eminent speech writers like Lysias, Isaeus and Demosthenes. And though many of the 'facts' presented to the jury were no doubt false, they must have been plausible, and therefore typical.

Isaeus in one of his speeches states that Dicaeogenes received an inheritance which brought in 80 minae a year as rent, but that he was never trierarch, though others served who owned less property (capital), than he received in rent (income).[40] Isaeus implies that a man might be a trierarch if he owned less than $1\frac{1}{3}$ talents, but one wonders whether if pressed he could have cited examples. In another speech Isaeus speaks of a '5 talent trierarchic fortune' as something worth having.[41] Five talents must have been well above the average trierarchic estate, for if it had been the average, the 1,200 men on the trierarchic register would between them have owned 1,200 x 5 = 6,000 talents, 'the whole assessment of Attica', leaving nothing at all for the other 4,800 eisphora payers. If the average trierarchic estate was only 3 talents, the total assessment of the 1,200 would have been 3,600 talents, leaving only 2,400 for the other eisphora payers, or only an average of ½ talent or 30 minae each. And an average of 3 talents means that the majority must have owned less than this amount, since a few are known to have owned considerably more. Isaeus' clients, who own fortunes ranging from 5½ or 5 talents, through 4, 3½, 3, 2½, down to 1½, seem to be a fairly representative cross-section of the richer members of the trierarchic register.⁴² Demosthenes, when he complains that other estates of one or two talents, by being leased during a minority, have been doubled or trebled, and so have become liable to liturgies, appears to be talking in a rather exaggerated vein, to impress upon the jury the magnitude of his own lost fortune.⁴³ Actually it would seem, an estate of 2 talents or less might well be on the trierarchic register.

There were of course richer men than this, who would be found among the Three Hundred, the leaders and second and third men (ἡγεμόνες, δεύτεροι, τρίτοι) of the 100 eisphora symmories. Here again no property qualification was required. The Three Hundred were the 300 richest men in Athens; they were enrolled by the generals, against whose choice an appeal lay to the courts by the process of *antidosis*.⁴⁴ Demosthenes in the speeches against Aphobus implies that an assessment of 15 talents brought a man within the highest schedule of eisphora payers, and that only a very few very rich men like Timotheus, the son of Conon, came within this class. His guardians, he alleged, had assessed him in this class, and had made him leader (ἡγεμών) of his symmory 'on no small assessments, but on such large ones that I paid 500 drachmae on 25 minae'. Whatever these much-disputed words mean, it is plain that Demosthenes implies that by no means all the 100 leaders of the symmories, much less the second and third members, who comprised the rest of the Three Hundred, had fortunes of 15 talents.[45]

In view of this it is wise to be sceptical about the very large figures quoted for some Athenian fortunes. Lysias in an interesting speech warns the jury against believing hearsay figures. The famous Nicias was reputed to possess 100 talents, but his son Niceratus only inherited 14. Ischomachus, the improving landlord who is the hero of Xenophon's *Oeconomicus*, was thought to be worth 70 talents, but cut up for only 20.[46] Some big fortunes were occasionally made. Conon did very well in the Great King's service and left 40 talents.[47] A lucky strike in the silver mines might yield fabulous wealth. The estate of Diphilus, a fortunate concessionnaire of Laurium, when confiscated by Lycurgus for breaches of the mining law, brought 160 talents into the treasury.[48] A certain Epicrates, who was lucky enough to sink a productive shaft outside the scheduled area at Laurium, was stated by an informer to have made (with his partners, 'pretty well all the richest men in the city') 300 talents in three years from this private mine, on which he paid no lease or royalty:[49] he was reputed by hearsay to have been later worth 600 talents.[50] But the largest fortune of which we have any authentic information is that of the banker Pasion, who left a shield factory with a net annual profit of 1 talent, 50 talents invested in loans, and land to the value of 20 talents—75 to 80 talents in all.[51]

Although fortunes such as these were quite exceptional, it does nevertheless seem to have been true that there was a heavy concentration of wealth at the extreme top of Athenian society, in a small group of approximately 300 families. Demosthenes at any rate thought so in the latter part of his career. He noted that under the existing trierarchic system the rich got off with a small expenditure, whereas citizens of moderate or small fortunes were being ruined. This was partly due to the unfair system (or lack of system), whereby everyone on the trierarchic register contributed equally, and not according to his means. But Demosthenes in his reform of the trierarchy did not merely make contributions vary according to property, with the result, as he says, that a rich man, who had hitherto got off with one-sixteenth of a trierarchy, was sometimes responsible for two entire ships.[52] He seems to have thrown the whole burden of the trierarchy on the Three Hundred, who were divided into twenty symmories of fifteen members.[53] This implies that he thought that three-quarters of the men on the trierarchic register were too poor to make, without undue hardship, a significant contribution to the fleet. Whereas he claims that the remaining quarter carried the burden easily, with the result that the efficiency of the navy was greatly improved.

Whence did the great families derive their wealth? The men whom I have already mentioned are not altogether typical. There were of course other Athenians besides Conon who made great fortunes as condottieri in the service of the Great King or his satraps, or of the rebel kings of Egypt, or the Thracian chieftains. There were other entrepreneurs besides Epicrates and Diphilus who made fortunes in the Laurium silver mines. Pasion is an exceptional case, for he was a slave by orign and a metic most of his life. He made his fortune in two ways typical of metics, by banking and by running a large-scale slave factory,[54] as Cephalus of Syracuse had done in an earlier generation:[55] he must have bought his land late in life when made a citizen. Demosthenes senior is also, to all appearances, rather peculiar in possessing a fortune consisting exclusively of two slave factories, and cash and investments, without a single acre of land.[56] One may suspect that he was a self-made man, for Demosthenes never alludes to his ancestors.

Timotheus, Conon's son, appears in Demosthenes' speeches as a considerable landlord, owning, besides an estate in the Plain, other properties which he could mortgage for 7 talents.[57] He possessed no great reserves of cash, for he was obliged to borrow from the banker Pasion, having already pledged his land. Pasion began late in life to move into land, and Apollodorus, his extravagant elder son, appears later as a considerable landlord, owning property in three demes,[58] but like Timotheus short of liquid assets. If these great fortunes had in the second generation been converted into land, it seems likely that the majority of the 300 families were in land. Xenophon's friend, Ischomachus, was certainly a diligent gentleman-farmer; and he left 20 talents.[59] Phaenippus, who ought to have been one of the Three Hundred by rights (according to a Demosthenic speech), owned one estate, which was by Athenian standards vast, over 40 stades (nearly 5 miles) in circumference. Only about a quarter can have been arable, for he did not raise much more than 1,000 medimni of barley: there were also vineyards which produced over 800 metretae of wine; but most of the estate seems to have been scrub, for Phaenippus employed six donkeys carrying firewood, and reckoned to make 12 drachmae a day by sales.[60] These facts may serve to remind us that even the richest Athenians were relatively modest men.

In the speeches of Isaeus half a dozen middle-class fortunes, ranging from just over 5 to just under 2 talents, are analysed in detail; Timarchus' estate, described by Aeschines, seems to fall into the same class. The pattern is very uniform. The main item is always a farm, or two small farms, sometimes with stock (that is, presumably worked by the owner), sometimes without stock (presumably let to a tenant). There is usually also house property, in Athens or in the demes; the urban property is sometimes a bath, or a brothel or a bar. Occasionally there is a little money invested, and sometimes a few industrial slaves: Euctemon had some craftsmen, Ciron some slaves who earned wages, Timarchus nine or ten leather workers who brought him in 2 obols a day each, and two other craftsmen.[61] There were no doubt Athenians in this class whose fortunes were differently balanced, who were mainly in loans or slaves. But we do not hear much of them. Socrates, as reported by Xenophon, cited five Athenians who lived mainly on industrial slaves, but of them he only claims that one performed liturgies—the others merely lived in a comfortable style.[62] One may suspect that the owners of industrial slaves were in general rather humble people, mainly no doubt successful craftsmen.

The large slave owner like Nicias does not appear in the fourth century, even in the mines.[63] The Laurium mines after the Decelean war were but little exploited for two generations, as we learn from Xenophon's *Vectigalia* and the fragmentary accounts of the *poletai*.[64] We hear during this time of some Athenian citizens working in the mines with their own hands. Among the prospective hirers of his projected public slaves, Xenophon distinguishes 'those who are themselves in the mines and are growing old', and 'others, who would not or could not work with their hands, but would gladly make their living as supervisors'.[65] A client of Demosthenes boasts: 'In earlier times I made a lot of money from the silver mines, working and toiling myself with my own hands.'[66] More often the Athenian who leased a mine worked it by slave labour; a high proportion of the recorded lessees are otherwise known as men of property. The numbers employed were not, however, necessarily large. We know of one lessee, Pantaenetus, who owned thirty slaves; these, with a workshop, were apparently his sole assets, for he raised money on this security to buy a concession.[67] The very wealthy mineowner Epicrates, who is said to have been worth 600 talents, had 'pretty well all the richest men in the city' in partnership with him early in his career, presumably because he needed their aid to buy and maintain enough slaves to exploit his mine.[68]

I have depicted a society in which, except for a small group of relatively very rich men at the top, and a larger group of casual labourers at the bottom, wealth was evenly distributed, and the graduation from the affluent to the needy very gentle. I have also depicted a society in which the great majority, from rich landowners down to peasants working a tiny allotment, derived most of their wealth from the land. This latter point cannot be fully substantiated, but apart from the evidence which I have given

above, it is favoured by a legal point. The ownership of land
(and house property) was a jealously guarded privilege of citizens,
very rarely granted to foreigners.[69] And there were a large
number of foreigners permanently domiciled in Attica—according to the census of Demetrius of Phalerum nearly half as many
as there were citizens—who were debarred from ownership of
land and houses, and had to make their living from industry and
commerce.

I do not of course suggest that there was an absolute dichotomy
between the activities of citizens and metics. Among the metics
enfranchised in 401 were a number of land workers ($\gamma\varepsilon\omega\varrho\gamma o\iota$),
not to speak of a gardener ($\varkappa\eta\pi o\nu\varrho\acute{o}\varsigma$); these were presumably
tenant farmers or agricultural labourers.[70] On the other hand we
know of one banker, Aristolochus, who was an Athenian—he is
recorded to have owned land;[71] of the other bankers known to
us a high proportion were certainly metics, mostly freedmen.[72]
We also know of two Athenian brothers, Diodotus and Diogei-
ton, who were merchants: the former left a fortune unlike any
other recorded for an Athenian—5 talents cash on deposit, and $7\frac{2}{3}$
talents invested in nautical loans.[73] Then there is Andocides, a
gentleman who went into trade during his exile,[74] and two or three
obscurer figures.[75] The other merchants and sea captains whom we
meet are, so far as we can trace their origin, foreigners,[76] and so
are nearly all those who financed them with nautical loans:
one of the exceptions here is Demosthenes senior, who had 70
minae—about a twelfth of his fortune—invested in these rather
speculative securities.[77] In industry metics do not seem to have
had so decisive a superiority, but the two largest factories known
both belonged to men of alien origin, one of over 100 hands to
Cephalus, a Syracusan, and another, which yielded a net annual
profit of a talent to Pasion, a freedman.[78]

The economic structure of Athenian society helps to explain
why the democracy, by contrast with other contemporary democracies, was at once so conservative and so stable. No suggestion
was ever put forward for the redistribution of the land ($\gamma\tilde{\eta}\varsigma$

ἀναδασμός) or for the cancellation of debts (χρεῶν ἀποκοπή), which more revolutionary democracies conducted. This is readily understandable in a society where property, and particularly land, was so widely distributed. Nor did 'the liberation of the slaves with revolutionary intent' (δούλων ἀπελευθέρωσις ἐπὶ νεωτερισμῷ), the third of the revolutionary perils against which Philip and Alexander guaranteed the cities of Greece under the League of Corinth,[79] ever occur at Athens. At times of national emergency the assembly was willing to free the slaves. To help man the fleet which won the battle of Arginusae all slaves of military age were called up with the promise (which was honoured) of freedom.[80] After the defeat of Chaeronea, Hyperides proposed and carried a motion to free the slaves for the defence of Athens, but when the crisis passed over, it was quashed and its author—unsuccessfully—prosecuted.[81] It is understandable that a full assembly, in which relatively few would be slave owners, might in a national emergency vote for the freeing of slaves; but normally respect for the rights of property prevailed.

The conservative tone of the Athenian democracy in its turn helps to account for its stability. In most contemporary states there was continuous class war, and counter-revolution alternated with revolution. In Athens from the establishment of the full democracy in 461 to its suppression by the Macedonian regent Antipater in 322 there were only two counter-revolutions, in 411 and 404; both were very short-lived, and the latter imposed by the victorious Spartan army and supported by a Spartan garrison. There was at all times a small group of wealthy intellectuals who hated the democracy, but in normal circumstances they found no support among the middle class of hoplites, or even in the upper trierarchic class. In 411, when the prestige of the democracy was deeply shaken by the Sicilian disaster, they did rally the middle and upper classes, resentful of the continued levies of eisphora and trierarchies which the long war was demanding, to the programme of the Five Thousand, a widely based oligarchy. But this constitutional experiment, which Thucydides praised highly, had a short life. In 404 again, when the war was lost, the Thirty at first enjoyed the support of the upper and middle classes, but they rapidly alienated it by their violent and arbitrary conduct. The result was that the bulk of the hoplite class fought on the democratic side in the civil war which followed, and that their leaders played a prominent part in the restoration of the democracy. Not even now were there reprisals or confiscations, and henceforth the democracy was un-challenged. In Athenian eyes democracy stood for the rule of law and the protection of property, as was natural when so many citizens were owners of property, and this fact reconciled to it the wealthier classes.

With an economy such as I have described, it may well be asked how Athens maintained its balance of payments with the rest of the world. It is unfortunately impossible even to begin to calculate exports and imports in figures. One can only point out first that payments must have balanced strictly, since there was no international credit system, and transactions were on a cash basis: and secondly that the bill for imports must have been very heavy. Imported corn alone, at the rate of 800,000 medimni per annum, at 5 drachmae, the normal price,[82] would have cost about 650 talents. There were other foodstuffs imported on a large scale, such as salt fish. Then there was timber, essential for housing and above all for shipbuilding, and for the latter purpose pitch, hemp and flax as well. Iron and bronze had all to be imported, both for home use and as raw material for export industries, not to speak of luxury materials for these latter, like the ivory which Demosthenes senior used to ornament his beds. Finally, slaves were nearly all imported.

On the other side there was one important agricultural export, olive oil: not much is heard of wine. Honey and figs, though noted for their quality, can hardly have been commercially signi-ficant items. Among industrial products Attic pottery is of course famous, and has perhaps, owing to its durability, unduly overshadowed other high-grade artistic products, such as silver plate and furniture. Something must be allowed for invisible exports—such as the profits of nautical loans paid in Athens, and the expenditure of visitors, commercial and others, in the city. But much of the bill was paid in cash, in drachmae minted from the Laurium silver, as is amply attested by the vast quantities of Athenian drachmae found in Thrace, the Bosporus, Asia Minor, Syria and Egypt. During the first half of the fourth century, when the mines were not very active, this resource must have been less important, but in the *Vectigalia* Xenophon can still claim that Athens attracts merchants because they can obtain payment for their goods in sound coin.[83] From about 340 silver production rose sharply, and the export of drachmae must have been considerable.

We today, wishing to sell our exports and to buy necessary imports of foodstuffs and raw materials, are acutely anxious about the sale of our exports, but have no worries about our imports, provided we can pay for them. The Athenians, in a similar position, were apparently unconscious of any export problem, but were greatly exercised by the danger of insufficient imports, particularly of corn. There were laws imposing drastic penalties on anyone resident at Athens, citizen or metic, who imported corn to any place save the Athenian market, and on anyone who lent money to finance a voyage which did not terminate at Athens.[84] Litigants take great pains to clear themselves of the imputation of having even intended to evade these laws, but reveal without any compunction to the jury that they have lent money to a shipper for a return voyage to Bosporus, on the express condition that he sail in ballast from the Peiraeus, and load wine at Mende or Scione for sale at Bosporus.[85] The kings of Bosporus are praised for expediting the export of corn from their dominions to Athens, and particularly for waiving the export tax;[86] it never apparently occurred to the Athenians that it would profit them if the import taxes at Bosporus on Athenian goods were abolished. Xenophon declares that merchants are popular everywhere, because 'all cities welcome as friends those who import things'.[87]

This attitude is partly explained by simple ignorance of economics. Every Athenian knew the unpleasant consequences when insufficient corn was shipped into the Peiraeus, and they took such obvious legal and administrative measures as lay within their power to force shippers to bring corn there. They were also aware of the periodic gluts of various Athenian products, but they attributed them to over-production, not to lack of markets. As Xenophon remarks, when there are a large number of bronze or iron workers, the price of their products goes down, and they are ruined: similarly when there is a large quantity of corn or wine grown, the price of crops goes down, agriculture becomes unprofitable, and many leave the land.[88]

The blindness of the Athenians may have been increased by the fact that a considerable proportion of imports was paid for in coin, minted from the silver mined in Attica, so that the sight of empty ships leaving the Peiraeus caused no alarm.[89] Secondly while all Athenians were consumers, and most of them producers of agricultural or industrial goods, very few were merchants. But whatever the reasons, it is a fact that the Athenians were blind to the importance of markets for their exports.

Some modern historians have read into Athenian foreign policy commercial motives, and attributed, for instance, the hostility of Athens and Corinth to a rivalry for markets. Such a view is, I would submit, quite unhistorical, It is possible to detect in Athenian foreign policy a desire to control by war or diplomacy the principal sources from which the city drew its supplies of corn and of timber, and the sea lanes along which these supplies had to travel. To such motives may be attributed Athens' interventions in Egypt and later in Sicily, and her sustained interest in the northern shores of the Pontus, her main source of corn, and in the Hellespont and the Bosporus, through which the Pontic cornships had to sail. Her anxiety for her supply of timber accounts for her persistent attempts to recover

Amphipolis, whose loss in 424 caused alarm 'because the city was useful to them both in the despatch of shipbuilding timber and in its money revenue'.[90] Even where the ancient sources, which often unduly neglect economic motives, are silent, it is not unreasonable from what we know of the Athenian people to postulate that they may have been influenced by anxiety for their essential imports. But that they were concerned about where merchants sold the goods that they bought from them there is no evidence at all.

V

HOW DID THE ATHENIAN DEMOCRACY WORK?

How did the Athenian Democracy Work?

ALCIBIADES once described the Athenian democracy as 'acknowledged folly',[1] and prima facie this would seem to be fair enough comment on a political system which entrusted most of the administration of the State to magistrates annually chosen by lot, and all political decisions to mass meetings which any citizen might—or might not—attend. Yet the fact remains that Athens was, by ancient standards, a remarkably efficient State, and that her foreign and domestic policy was directed as well as, if not better than, that of contemporary cities with what might seem to be more sensible constitutions.

To deal with administration first, the Athenian army was only average, by no means up to Spartan standards, and from the middle of the fifth century surpassed by the Boeotian. It was ill disciplined. This was especially true of the cavalry, which consisted of wealthy and usually aristocratic youths,[2] and this though the Athenians spent a great deal of money—about 40 talents a year—on it,[3] and devoted much attention to it. There were not only the two elected commanders of the cavalry and the elected commanders of the tribal squadrons.[4] There was an elective board of ten who enrolled the troopers, and the council annually checked the list and inspected the horses.[5] Yet Xenophon's little treatise on the duties of a cavalry commander reveals how slack and indisciplined the corps was.

The 'Old Oligarch' accounted for the inefficiency of the army as being due to the fact that the Athenians, a naval people, took no pride in it.[6] Socrates explained it partly by the sense of inferiority caused by the defeats at Lebadeia and Delium; and Periclean strategy must have lowered Athenian military morale.

But curiously enough he found the main explanation in amateur generals.[7] Yet all the higher military officers were elected, and the lower grades nominated,[8] and no ancient city—not even Rome—conceived any better way of choosing a general than by popular election.

The navy was on the other hand indisputably of high efficiency, although commanded by the same generals, and although administered by other bodies even less likely to be competent. The council was responsible for building as many triremes as the people ordered each year, and delegated the task to an elective sub-committee of ten. The naval architects were elected by the people.[9] The superintendents of the dockyards, who saw to the maintenance of the ships and their tackle, were probably one of the usual boards of ten chosen by lot.[10] When a fleet was to be commissioned an *ad hoc* board of ten was elected to organise the process.[11] The trierarchs, who were, as it would seem, the key men, being responsible for training the crews, maintaining the ships in fighting efficiency and actually commanding them at sea, were merely rich citizens serving in rotation.[12] The trierarchic system had its weaknesses: there were inefficient or niggardly trierarchs, and in the fourth century some who handed over their responsibilities to contractors.[13] But on the whole trierarchs, despite grumbling at the expense, seem to have taken a pride in their ships, stimulated by prizes.[14] They personally, of course, had not the skill to train their crews or navigate their ships, but they paid bonuses to attract skilled petty officers—steersmen, boatswains and the like—and good rowers, especially the top bench men.[15] It was the existence of a large pool of such experienced seamen—and shipwrights—among the citizens which gave the Athenian navy its unique efficiency.[16]

Another department of the administration which was indisputably very efficiently run was the religious festivals, including dramatic, musical and athletic displays; an Athenian chorus was, Socrates admits, unrivalled.[17] The festivals were directed partly by magistrates or boards chosen by lot, partly by elective boards,[18]

but the main responsibility fell on the choregi, who like the
trierarchs were rich citizens serving in rotation.[19] As with the
trierarchs, their function, which they usually performed with
zealous emulation, was to furnish money. Antisthenes, a rich
man who had repeatedly been choregus and won the prize
every time, 'though knowing nothing about music or the training of choirs, still was able to secure the best men in these fields'.[20]
The excellence of the performances depended on the existence of
a pool of highly skilled trainers and dancers and singers, for whose
services choregi competed.[21]

More surprisingly finance, both imperial and domestic, was
tolerably efficient, though this department was run entirely by
boards chosen by lot, supervised by the council, until, in the
latter half of the fourth century, an elective treasurer of the military fund and elective managers of the theoric fund were created.[22]
There was a great multiplicity of financial magistrates, whose
functions are explained in Aristotle's Constitution of Athens. A
brief description of peace-time domestic finance—the war tax is
discussed in another chapter—[23] may suffice to illustrate the system.

There were ten treasurers ($\tau\alpha\mu\acute{\iota}\alpha\iota$) of the sacred moneys of
Athena,[24] and from 434 until the middle of the fourth century
ten treasurers of the sacred moneys of the other Gods:[25] these
boards were combined from 406 to 386. They were mere
accountants who kept the books and received and paid out money
on order from the people. These accounts were used in the fifth
century as reserve funds, into which surpluses were paid, and
from which money could be borrowed by the people for extra-
ordinary expenses.[26] There were the auditors ($\lambda o\gamma\iota\sigma\tau\alpha\acute{\iota}$),
thirty in the fifth century, ten with ten advocates to assist them
in the fourth, who audited the accounts of all magistrates who
had handled public money,[27] and in addition an audit committee
of the council (chosen by lot from its own number) which checked
all such accounts every prytany.[28]

The ordinary internal revenue consisted on the one hand of
sundry taxes, rents of public and sacred lands, and mining royal-

ties and concession prices, and on the other hand of fees, fines and confiscations imposed by the courts.[29] Fines were collected by a board of Exactors (πράκτορες) on the instructions of the presidents of the courts.[30] The items in the first group were all farmed by a board of ten, the Sellers (πωληταί): the auctions were held in the presence of the council, which selected the concessionaires by vote: confiscated estates were similarly sold by auction. The Sellers had to make out forms showing what payments were due from concessionaires and purchasers and at what dates, and their business was then finished.[31] Another board, the ten Receivers (ἀποδέκται), were responsible for receiving the payments due, granting receipts (by deleting the demand forms drawn up by the Sellers) in the presence of the council, and reporting defaulters to the council (which could imprison them).

The Receivers also made every prytany an allocation of the funds received to the spending departments.[32] This was, so long as funds sufficed, a purely mechanical process, as certain fixed sums were allocated by law or by decree of the people for various purposes. Thus the assembly itself had a petty cash account of 10 talents a year to pay for engraving inscriptions, presenting crowns to deserving persons, supplying journey money to ambassadors, entertaining foreign envoys and the like.[33] The council had a similar fund,[34] and so did various boards of magistrates, such as the wardens of the market (ἀγορανόμοι)[35] and the managers of the Dionysia and the repairers of the temples—the two last had fixed allocations of 100 and 30 minas a year respectively.[36] Most of these funds had their separate treasurers—the treasurer of the people, the treasurer of the council,[37] the treasurer of the board for trireme construction[38] and so forth.

The allocation by the Receivers caused trouble only when funds were inadequate. The regular receipts were rather seasonal, the great majority falling due on the ninth prytany, and receipts from fees, fines and confiscations were of course very variable.[39] Moreover at some periods, notably the early years of the fourth century, the gross receipts were barely adequate to cover statutory

expenditure. In some circumstances some expenses might have
to be cut; Lysias complains of Nicomachus that, by increasing
the number of statutory public sacrifices, he had caused ancient
sacrifices to the amount of 3 talents to be omitted,[40] and Demosthenes envisages the possibility of sessions of the council and the
assembly and the courts being suspended for lack of pay[41]—
during the Euboean crisis of 348 the courts were apparently
suspended for this reason.[42] On the other hand, as Lysias reveals,
the council was in these circumstances tempted to welcome
informations laid against wealthy citizens, in the hope of large
fines or confiscations.[43] From his remarks, and the account in
Aristotle of the functions of the Receivers, it would seem that
the council took ultimate responsibility for balancing receipts
and expenditure somehow.

The system seems unnecessarily complicated, with its many
boards, each dealing with one stage of the process. The object
probably was to make peculation or improper expenditure of
public funds or slackness in exacting State dues difficult by making
the money and accounts pass through many hands. The system
was also excessively rigid, allowing for very little give and take
except by special decree of the people. Thus, when ships had to
be built in an emergency in 407-6, the people had to decree that
the generals should borrow the money required from the Receivers and pay it to the shipwrights, to be repaid in due course
by the board for trireme construction, whose vote was presumably exhausted.[44] Again in 343 when the people wished to
give a pension of a drachma a day to an exiled Delian, Peisitheides, they paid the amount from the petty cash fund of the
assembly, but, to put the payment on a regular footing, had to
give instructions that on the next meeting of the legislative
assembly it be added to the authorised payments made by the
treasurer of the people.[45] Similarly in 329 when new sacrifices
were voted to Amphiaraus, pending the next meeting of the
legislative assembly the money had to be lent by the treasurer of
the people.[46]

It was, however, this minute subdivision of duties and rigid regulation that made it possible for such complicated business as finance to be conducted by annual boards chosen by lot, that is by any citizen (over 30 years of age) who had sufficient confidence in himself to face the preliminary scrutiny and the more searching examination of his record which would terminate his year's office.[47]

All the evidence, from the Old Oligarch to Demosthenes and Aristotle,[48] indicates that, perhaps with the exception of the old archonships,[49] which demanded by tradition expenditure in excess of the meagre pay, and had some rather exacting duties, like the choice of dramatists to compete at the Dionysia, the offices chosen by lot were filled by quite humble citizens. In these circumstances a permanent civil service was hardly needed. There was a public slave who assisted the Sellers and Receivers. He had custody of the payment notes made by the former (no doubt under his guidance) and produced them for the latter at the appropriate dates, and received back for custody the cancelled notes when payment had been made.[50] There were also some semi-professional secretaries or under-secretaries of boards. The important secretaries were either chosen by lot, like the secretary of the Nine Archons[51] or the secretary of the council 'over the laws,' or elected, like the secretary of the council and people 'by the prytany', who recorded decrees; but by Aristotle's day even the last was chosen by lot, and only the secretary who read documents to the council and people was—for obvious reasons—elected.[52] Secretaries of minor boards of magistrates were, however, generally hired by them, as were under-secretaries. The men who occupied these posts were humble folk, even, like Nicomachus, freedmen,[53] and generally despised. Demosthenes never let Aeschines forget that in his poverty-stricken youth he had earned his living as 'secretary and attendant of petty magistracies' and as under-secretary of the council and people.[54] Such men, no doubt, acquired a knowledge of routine which was useful to their chiefs, but lest they should acquire too much influence it was laid down that no under-secretary might serve the same board more than once.[55]

Any decisions which rose above the level of routine were made by the council, which, as Aristotle reiterates, co-operated in most of the administrative work of the magistrates.[56] The council also, as we have seen, did some important work itself, either in full session or through committees. It was in fact the co-ordinating body which held the administrative machine together. But it had a second and more important function, that of steering committee of the assembly. By a rule which was very rarely broken, no decision might be taken by the assembly except on a probouleuma, a motion voted by the council, and placed by the council on the agenda.[57] This brings us to the means by which political decisions were arrived at. But first we must consider the composition and the procedure of the council and of the assembly.

The council of 500 was chosen annually by lot, 50 from each tribe.[58] Places were allocated to each deme of Athens and Attica in rough proportion to their importance, and the allotment took place in the demes.[59] Like magistrates councillors had to be over thirty years of age,[60] to take an oath,[61] and to submit individually to preliminary scrutiny[62] and final examination:[63] it may be conjectured that technically they had, like magistrates, to be of at least zeugite census. From these features, and in particular the elaborately representative structure of the council, it has been inferred that in the original Cleisthenic constitution it was intended to be the effective governing body of the State, only referring major and contentious issues to the people.[64] If so, it very soon ceased to be so. From the fact that it was chosen by lot, with the further provision that no one might serve on it more than two years in his life,[65] it is clear that the Athenians of the fifth and fourth centuries intended that the council should have no chance of developing a corporate sense, which would enable it to take an independent line, and wished it to be merely a fair sample of the Athenian people, whose views would naturally coincide with those of the people.

There was never any difficulty in filling the council, so far as we know. Even when the population was low in the latter part of the fourth century, the ephebe classes, which comprised citizens of 18 or 19 of hoplite status, averaged about 500, which means, as the table on page 82 will make clear, that the 30-year-old class each year would number from 400 to 350; so that with some few serving twice the council could have been manned from hoplites alone.[66] There are fairly strong indications that in the fourth century the council contained many well-to-do members—though it cannot be proved that no poor men sat on it. There are moreover suggestions that a man who wanted to get on in a given year had a good chance of doing so.[67] Demosthenes served a very crucial year, and Aeschines declares 'at this point Demosthenes entered the council chamber as a councillor, without having drawn the lot as a member or as a reserve, but by scheming corruption'.[68] This is no doubt a lie, but combined with the statement of Aristotle that the allotment of other magistracies had to be removed from the demes because they sold them, it does suggest that in some poor demes at any rate there were not many applicants for the seats, and that the demesmen were not unwilling to arrange for a generous carpet-bagger to be selected.[69] All this suggests that few poor men put down their names, and that competition for places was therefore rather slack.

It is not known why the poor liked serving in magistracies rather than on the council. Perhaps a magistracy better satisfied a craving for a spell of importance and authority, which being one of 500 councillors did not. At the same time the duties of a councillor were, in theory at any rate, exacting. The council sat every day except on festivals. The tribes took the presidency (prytany) in rotation (by lot) for a tenth of the year (thirty-five or thirty-six days), known therefore as a prytany. The members of the presiding tribe had to dine every day in the city hall, and summoned the council and assembly.[70]

From their number was drawn daily by lot the foreman (ἐπιστάτης) of the presidents, who for twenty-four hours had custody of the common seal of the city and the keys of the temples where the archives and moneys were stored. He was assisted by one-third of the presiding tribe whom he selected. In the fifth century he also served as chairman of the council and assembly (if one was held on his day). In the fourth he selected by lot from the other nine tribes of the council nine chairmen (πρόεδροι), and out of them a foreman of the chairman. No citizen might be foreman of the presidents more than once (so that thirty-five or thirty-six out of the fifty had to serve), and in the fourth century no chairman might serve more than once in a prytany, and no foreman of the chairmen more than once in the year.[71]

These rules are an interesting commentary on the Athenian preference for democracy over efficiency. Rather than have a chairman who might exercise undue influence on the council or the assembly they were prepared to risk having one who could not distinguish between an amendment and a substantive motion. Such inexperienced chairmen might even be a danger. According to Aeschines 'some people easily propose illegal decrees and others put them to the vote without being allotted the chairmanship in the straightforward way, but taking the chair in an underhand fashion (he does not explain how this was done, but presumably by persuading one's colleagues to abstain from the ballot), and if one of the other councillors does genuinely ballot and is allotted to be chairman . . . they threaten to lay an information against him, bullying the ordinary members'.[72]

The high odds on being placed in this position of terrifying prominence may help to account for the reluctance of the humble to serve on the council. For a foreman was not only exposed to jeers and groans, but to penalties if he put an illegal motion to the vote, or otherwise broke standing orders. It will be remembered how Nicias, in the second debate of the Sicilian expedition, urged the foreman to break the rules by allowing the question of the expedition to be reopened although already voted upon, and encouraged him by saying that to break the rules in so good a

cause could not bring down punishment.[73] The final responsibility on such points of order was however apparently shared by
all the presidents (in the fifth century) or chairmen (in the fourth).
Socrates happened to be one of the presidents at the debate on
the ten generals and courageously protested against putting the
illegal motion of the council to the vote, but was overruled;[74] so
was Demosthenes when he was one of the chairmen on a less
famous occasion.[75]

In practice attendance at the council seems to have been
rather slack, in the fourth century at any rate. Demosthenes
in one passage draws a distinction between the active minority
on the council, the politicians, who make speeches and propose
motions, and the ordinary members, who 'keep their mouths
shut and propose no motions, and perhaps don't even enter the
council chamber as a rule'.[76]

The assembly had four regular meetings every prytany, or
forty in the year. The agenda for them was to some extent
fixed by law. Thus on the first of the four a vote had to be taken
whether to continue the magistrates in office or depose any of
them: next the corn supply and the security of the country had
to be discussed; next lists of confiscated property and of heiresses
were read, and an opportunity was given for bringing motions
of censure against informers, or laying information against
traitors or denouncing those who had failed to fulfil their promises to the people. The second meeting was devoted to what
may be called private members' business, when anyone might
speak to the poeple on any topic of private or public interest.
The other two dealt with current problems under the headings
of sacred affairs, foreign policy and secular affairs, with priority
for three motions (selected by lot) on each topic in that order of
precedence.[77] Besides the regular assemblies there were special
meetings. These might be summoned to deal with some sudden
emergency—Aeschines was presumably thinking of such meetings when he declared that owing to Demosthenes' disastrous
foreign policy there had of late been more special than regular

assemblies.[78] They might also be arranged beforehand to allow
a full debate on an important issue. Thus when it had been
resolved to assist the Segestans and Leontines at one assembly,
a second was called at only four days' interval to discuss the
details of the expedition, and two assemblies (on successive days)
were set aside to discuss the Peace of Philocrates.[79]

How large and how regular attendance at the assembly was,
it is difficult to say. The oligarchs in 411, defending the constitution of the 5,000, declared to the democrats at Samos, 'that
owing to military service and business overseas more than 5,000
Athenians had never yet assembled to debate any question however important.'[80] This refers to the war years, in which many
Athenians were on active service, and is a tendentious statement:
it suggests that normal peace-time attendance may have been
well over 5,000. This conclusion is supported by the fact that a
quorum of 6,000 was required not only for ostracism,[81] but for
some quite unexciting issues, such as grants of citizenship,[82] or
special leave to propose a motion for remission of public debts,[83]
and that there is no hint that the quorum was ever not forth-
coming—though it was perhaps on these occasions that the
Scythian police literally roped people into the assembly.[84]

The social composition of the assembly is also difficult to
gauge. Socrates speaks of the assembly as composed of fullers,
shoemakers, carpenters, smiths, peasants, merchants and shopkeepers.[85] On the other hand, as I have argued in another chapter, the assemblies which Demosthenes addressed seem generally
to have been predominantly middle or upper class—hoplites
and payers of war tax.[86] Special meetings must have attracted
a larger working-class attendance. It was no doubt to such a
meeting that Demosthenes addressed the speech on the Symmories, where alone he appears to be facing an assembly of poor
men, who might recklessly vote a heavy war tax.[87] The assemblies on the Peace of Philocrates must also have contained a large
element of the poorer citizens, or Eubulus' intervention, that
rejection of the peace would mean both war tax and transfer

of the theoric money to the military fund, would not have been so effective.[88]

Demosthenes gives a moving description of the special assembly summoned when Philip occupied Elatea.[89] 'It was evening when a messenger came to the presidents with the news that Elatea was captured. They immediately got up in the middle of dinner and expelled the occupants of the stalls in the market place and burnt the hurdles, while others sent for the generals and summoned the trumpeter: and the city was full of tumult. The next day, at dawn, the presidents summoned the council to the council chamber, and you went to the assembly, and before the council had opened proceedings and voted a resolution the whole people was sitting up on the Pnyx. And then the council came in and the presidents announced the news that had been brought to them, and introduced the messenger, and he spoke. Then the herald asked: "Who wishes to speak?" And no one came forward.'

But perhaps the most vivid picture of the assembly's formal procedure is the charming skit in the Thesmophoriazusae:[90] the genuine nucleus can be readily separated from the comic additions and alterations. The session opens with a bidding prayer proclaimed by the female herald. 'Let there be silence! Let there be silence! Ye shall pray to the Thesmophorae, Demeter and the Maiden, and to Plutus and to Calligeneia, and to Earth the foster mother, and to Hermes and the Graces, that this present assembly and meeting may act for the best for the weal of the city of Athens, and for our own good: and that she who acts and speaks the best for the people of Athens, and womankind, may prevail. This ye shall pray, and for good to yourselves.' There follows a long curse. 'Ye shall pray to the Olympian and Pythian and Delian gods and goddesses, and to the other gods, that whosoever shall plot evil against the people of womankind, or shall negotiate with Euripides or the Persians to the harm of womankind, or shall plan to be a tyrant or to restore a tyrant (there follows a catalogue of sins especially offensive to womankind),

may he perish miserably and all his house; and ye shall pray
that the gods give good to all the rest of you.' Business now
begins. 'Listen all. The council of womankind has resolved as
follows. Timoclea was foreman: Lysilla was secretary: Sostrate
proposed the motion: "That an assembly be held on the middle
day of the Thesmophoria in the morning, when we all have
most leisure, and that the first item on the agenda be: what
should be done to Euripides, since it is evident that he wrongs us
all." Who wishes to speak?'

For the way in which decisions were reached in the council
and assembly we have three main sources, the descriptions of
famous debates in the historians, Thucydides and Xenophon;
the speeches of the orators, chiefly Demosthenes and Aeschines,
defending their own and denouncing their adversaries' political
tactics; and the inscriptions which record actual decrees. The
principal questions to be asked are: What were the respective
roles of the council and the assembly? Did the assembly merely
rubber-stamp resolutions worked out in detail in the council,
or did it make the real decisions and even in effect exercise the
initiative? And secondly, within the council and the assembly
respectively, how far could and did the ordinary citizen take the
initiative, and how far did political leaders, official or unofficial,
monopolise the tribune?

We may take the inscriptions first, as the most authentic
records. Fifth and early fourth century inscriptions are relatively
uninformative because they are too concisely drafted. The
official record gives only what is essential. The prescript merely
states: 'It was resolved by the council and people', and gives
the names of the presiding tribe and its foreman (since both were
in some measure responsible for putting the decree to the vote),
that of the secretary (who kept the minute of the decree and was
charged with having it correctly engraved) and that of the proposer (who might be prosecuted for moving an illegal decree):
the name of the archon is sometimes added (for the date). There
follows (in indirect speech) the text of the decree, usually with

nothing to show whether it was drafted by the council or in the assembly.

The only exceptions which are informative are amendments, which, if in the form: 'So and so proposed: Otherwise as resolved by the council; but that . . .', reveal that the original motion was drafted in the council, and put forward in its name. By this test it is possible to determine that several important fifth-century decrees were drafted in detail in council, and passed with minor modifications by the people. They include the alliance with Egesta of c. 458, the great reassessment of the tribute in 425, the privileges granted to Neapolis for its loyalty, the honours voted to the assassins of Phrynichus in 409, and the privileges given to the loyal Samians in 405 and 403: one of the last decrees is unique in being formally moved from the chair by the whole body of presidents, presumably to emphasise the council's unanimity.[91]

Some interesting points of detail arise from these decrees. The same man who had proposed a motion in the council might amend it in the assembly.[92] The council might draft a complex resolution, leaving some contentious clause or clauses open for the people to decide. Thus the council proposed various honours for Neapolis, but resolved that the question of whether the 'first fruits' should be reserved to Athena be left for discussion in the assembly. The assembly, in the form of an amendment, voted that they should.[93] In the decree about the assassins of Phrynichus the mover of the amendment not only suggested supplementary honours but instructed the council, if the principal honorand should (at a future date) ask for further privileges, to draft a resolution and bring it before the people.[94] This is an indication of how the people, in a very small way, could circumvent the rule of the probouleuma and take the initiative.

Conversely, when an amendment opens with the words 'otherwise as moved by so and so', it may reasonably be inferred that the substantive motion was not a probouleuma, but had been moved in the assembly by the citizen named. On this assumption some important decrees had not been drafted in the council. The regulations for the colony of Brea were proposed by its official founder, Democleides; the rules for the Eleusinian first fruits by a special board of draftsmen.[95] One of the decrees dealing with the settlement of Chalcis after its revolt in 446 was moved by a certain Anticles. That he made his proposal in the assembly is further suggested by a clause 'that the people forthwith (αὐτίκα μάλα) elect five men to go to Chalcis and administer the oath'. The word 'forthwith' is more natural in the mouth of a speaker in the assembly, where the vote could be taken straight away, than in that of a speaker in the council proposing action in an assembly to be held perhaps several days hence.[96]

If this last point is valid the first decree conferring various privileges on Methone in 428 was proposed by a citizen, Diopeithes, in the assembly.[97] It opens with the clause 'that the people forthwith vote with regard to the Methonaeans whether the people wishes forthwith to assess tribute or if it is enough for them to pay only what accrued to the Goddess from the tribute which they were assessed to pay at the last Panathenaea, and to be immune from the rest'. The decree goes on to confer various favours on Methone. At the end there is a note: 'the people voted that the Methonaeans pay only what accrued to the Goddess from the tribute which they were assessed to pay at the last Panathenaea, and be immune from the rest'. The words 'forthwith', twice used, again suggest a speaker in the assembly: when the council in their probouleuma about Neapolis left a similar decision to a special vote of the people they used a different formula: 'and about the first fruits for the Parthenos, which were even then paid to the Goddess, that the matter be considered in the people with regard to them'.[98]

The reason, it may be suggested, why Diopeithes formulated his proposal in this curiously cumbersome way may have been that amendments were not taken, as in modern practice, before the motion. In that case the whole motion might be jeopardised by one contentious clause, and a prudent politician therefore reserved such a clause for a special vote to be taken immediately after the main motion had been passed.

Early in the fourth century the formula of the prescript begins to be varied. In many decrees, it is still, as in the fifth century, 'it was resolved by the council and people', but in others it is 'it was resolved by people'.[99] Usually the first formula appears to be used when the people adopted the resolution of the council, and the second when the decree was moved in the assembly, but it is doubtful if this distinction was always strictly observed. It was technically correct to use the formula 'it was resolved by the council and people' in all cases, as was done in the fifth century, since no decree could be passed unless the council had passed a resolution putting the matter on the agenda; and in some cases the old practice seems to have been maintained.[100] Moreover no great importance seems to have attached to the formula and secretaries were sometimes careless. There are one or two decrees which must have been passed by the assembly but are headed 'it was resolved by the council';[101] presumably the secretary had forgotten to alter the prescript of the council's resolution when it was adopted by the people. In other cases the formula of enactment 'it was resolved by the (council and) people', is omitted altogether:[102] it cannot have been considered of vital significance.

Towards the end of the fifth century the drafting of decrees becomes less economical, and therefore more instructive to us. What evidently happened was this. Although in the stereotyped formula of the prescript the mover or amender of a motion is always said to speak, and in the technical language of the law was called the speaker (ῥήτωρ), motions and amendments were actually handed in in writing to the secretary, who read them aloud. The orators normally use the verb 'to write' for to move a resolution, and Aeschines tells a story which vividly illustrates the procedure: Demosthenes, he says, at an assembly showed to one of his neighbours 'a decree written by himself, with the name Demosthenes written on it', and asked whether he should give it to the secretary for the chairmen to put it to the vote.[103] If the motion, with or without amendments, were passed, the secretary seems to have handed over the papers without revision to the engraver to inscribe. A rather comic result of this slovenly procedure is seen in a decree granting the title of proxenos and benefactor in 408-7 to one Oeniades of Palaesciathos.[104] In the council's resolution he had been described as 'of Sciathos': an amendment was passed 'to alter "of Sciathos" to read "Oeniades of Palaesciathos"'; and this is solemnly engraved, although the correction has been made in the substantive motion.

An even more flagrant case of slovenly drafting is a decree passed on the motion of Cephisophon in favour of the Samians in 403.[105] It contains the provision 'that the embassy of the Samians be introduced to the people to deal with their requirements', which is clearly a purely procedural clause of the probouleuma, which should have been deleted when it was adopted by the people. Among the other provisions are 'that all the privileges which the people of the Athenians previously voted to the people of the Samians be confirmed', and an invitation of the embassy to dinner in the prytaneum. The main decree is followed by an amendment, also proposed by Cephisophon, 'that it has been voted by the people of the Athenians that the previous decrees about the Samians be confirmed, as the council resolved in its probouleuma and introduced to the people', and a second invitation of the embassy to dinner. It is difficult to see what to make of this muddle. Did the council forget to record in its probouleuma a resolution which it had passed confirming the earlier decrees and omit to invite the embassy to dinner? And did Cephisophon in his amendment correct these errors? And were the corrections embodied in the decree, as well as being recorded as an amendment?

A more revealing form of carelessness is to leave in the text of the decree the words (in indirect speech) 'it has been resolved by the council' or 'by the people', in addition to the statement in the prescript 'it was resolved by the (council and) people'.

This is a much more useful clue than the wording of the prescript. For a man moving a resolution in the council would never
begin with the words: 'it is resolved by the people,' nor a speaker
in the assembly with the words 'it is resolved by the council'.

In the 370s began a yet more slovenly practice. After the
standard prescript including the words 'it was resolved by the
council and people,' many decrees are drafted on such lines as
this: 'With regard to the statement made by the envoys from ——
that it is resolved by the council that the chairmen who shall by
lot preside at the next assembly shall introduce them to the
people and shall communicate a resolution of the council to the
people that the council resolves that, whereas, etc.'[106] What has
happened is that the whole probouleuma has been copied verbatim, and in these cases it is manifest that the assembly merely
rubber-stamped it.

A unique decree of 333 B.C. reveals a very different procedure.[107] After a prescript ending with the words: 'it was resolved
by the council: Antidotus son of Apollodorus of Sypalettus proposed,' is a probouleuma instructing the chairmen of the next
assembly to introduce the Citian delegation to the assembly and
'to communicate a resolution of the council to the people that the
council resolves that the people, having heard the Citians about
the foundation of the temple and any other Athenian who wishes,
shall decide as it thinks best'. There follows a second prescript
(in the next prytany) ending 'it was resolved by the people:
Lycurgus son of Lycophron proposed', and the decree of the
people (incorporating the words 'it was resolved by the people')
granting the request of the Citians.

This decree is unique in preserving such a non-committal
probouleuma: the reason probably is that the Citians engraved
it themselves (the secretary is not instructed to do so), and thought
it safest to have the whole dossier of documents inscribed as it
was handed to them by the secretary. But there are many decrees identical in form with the second half of the Citian decree.
Not all such decrees presuppose a purely non-committal probou-

leuma. A decree granting honours and privileges to one Archippus begins 'that it has been resolved by the people' but its preamble runs 'with regard to the statement of Archippus and the probouleuma which the council passed about him'.[108] Here it may be conjectured that the council had endorsed Archippus' claims and suggested in general terms that the people award him suitable honours, and that a speaker in the assembly made concrete proposals. Another decree, accepting the proffered alliance of Arcadia, Achaea, Elis and Phlius,[109] is also presented in the form of a motion in the assembly, 'that it has been resolved by the people', and opens with the proposal that the herald shall forthwith (in the assembly) pray for the blessing of the Gods on the alliance; but the preamble recites that 'the allies have introduced a resolution into the council to receive the alliance', and that 'the council have passed a probouleuma to the same effect'. Here it would seem that the council had made a firm recommendation. The speaker in the assembly may have formulated the exact terms of the alliance, or may have merely redrafted the council's motion, prefixing it with the proposal for a solemn prayer and an explanatory preamble.

As a rule, however, it would seem that if the probouleuma was adopted, it was engraved *totidem verbis*, with amendments, if any, subjoined; and it is therefore probable that decrees which open with the words 'that it has been resolved by the people' were for the most part, like that of Lycurgus on the Citians, proposed in the assembly on the basis of a purely formal probouleuma.

Using these clues it is often possible to distinguish when the initiative came from the council and when it left the assembly a free choice. The decree in favour of Clazomenae in 387 B.C. would seem to have been drafted by Poliagros in the assembly.[110] This decree, like that of Diopeithes on Methone, reserves some points for a special vote of the people: 'and about a governor and a garrison that the people decide forthwith whether they be established in Clazomenae or whether the people of Clazomenae be authorised to decide whether they wish to receive them or not'. At the end is a note: 'the people voted that they pay no other taxes (than the 5 per cent. mentioned in the decree) and receive neither garrison nor governor'.

It also appears that the alliances with Chios and Byzantium, immediately before the formation of the second Athenian League, and the foundation charter of the League itself, were drafted in the assembly.[111] On the other hand, subsequent accessions to the League were handled by the council, whose resolutions the people confirmed.[112]

The general conclusion which emerges from the inscriptions is that the council was not a policy-making body. On uncontentious matters it drafted decrees, sometimes leaving minor difficulties to be settled by the people, but on any major issue, and some minor ones, it merely put the question on the agenda of the assembly. This conclusion is borne out by the reports of debates in Thucydides. All the great issues were debated in the assembly and decided there, the Corcyraean alliance, the rejection of the Spartan ultimatum in 431, the fate of Mitylene, the Spartan overtures in 425 and again in 420, the Sicilian expedition.[113] The role of the council is rarely so much as mentioned, though of course it must have introduced the envoys. Only in 420 do we hear of the Spartan envoys going first to the council, and then to the assembly, where by a trick of Alcibiades they disowned the plenipotentiary powers which they had claimed before the council, and so enabled Alicibiades to discredit them.

In Xenophon's story of the trial of the ten generals the council plays a bigger part. The generals reported to the council, which on the motion of Timocrates imprisoned them and brought them before the assembly. After a long and rather inconclusive debate, in which the generals took part, the assembly, as it was getting too dark to count votes, decided to postpone the question and instructed the council to produce a probouleuma on how they should be tried. The enemies of the generals now took advantage of the fact that one of their number, Callixenus, was on the council. He made an attack on the generals and got a probouleuma passed that the people should vote for or against the death sentence on all without further debate, as the case had been fully discussed already. At the assembly, however, protests were raised and Euryptolemus proposed a rival motion. The people then voted between the probouleuma and Euryptolemus' motion, and after a recount adopted the former. This narrative incidentally reveals another procedural possibility. Even if the council made a definite recommendation, it could not only be amended: a quite different motion might be substituted.[114]

The orators do not add greatly to our knowledge. They confirm that vital decisions were left entirely to the assembly. In the debate on the peace of Philocrates there was apparently no substantive probouleuma before the assembly: by the procedure proposed by Demosthenes, on the first day any citizen might speak and propose a motion, on the second the motions were to be put to the vote.[115] It is clear from Demosthenes' narrative that on the capture of Elatea the council had no proposals to make, and left it to the assembly to produce them. At the same time the orators show that it might be tactically convenient to get a question raised through a friend on the council; thus Demosthenes probably used Apollodorus to move a probouleuma on the allocation of the surplus to the theoric and military funds.[116] Demosthenes also mentions a case, which by the nature of things could not be recorded on stone, where a probouleuma was rejected by the assembly. When the news of the disaster of Tamynae arrived the council passed a resolution that all the rest of the cavalry be sent to the front. At the assembly Meidias, to evade active service as a trooper, volunteered to be a trierarch 'before even the chairmen had taken their seats', but after debate it was decided not to mobilise the cavalry.[117]

Turning to the question of individual initiative, it is already plain that if, as often, the council made a noncommittal probouleuma any citizen could move a decree on the subject in the assembly, and that if they made a definite recommendation, any citizen could propose amendments, an alternative motion or outright rejection. It remains to consider however whether, and if so how, a citizen could get a question on to the agenda. The probouleuma rule did at least mean that no decree could be passed in the assembly unless the council had passed a formal resolution introducing the topic, and what evidence there is confirms the natural hypothesis that only a councillor could move a motion in council. The orators imply this by their language: 'Apollodorus, being a member of the council, moved a decree in the council and brought forward a probouleuma in the assembly',[118] or again: 'Timarchus, being a councillor, moved that . . .'.[119] The clearest evidence comes from Demosthenes' activities at the time of the negotiations which led up to the Peace of Philocrates. He was during the earlier stages on the council, and used his position to move various minor decrees—that the first Athenian envoys be crowned, that Philip's envoys be introduced to the people and that they be allocated seats in the theatre, that the second Athenian envoys sail forthwith[120]—but later, when his year was over, he cites 'the probouleuma which the council voted on my report and the testimony of its mover'.[121]

In practice no doubt a politician normally saw to it that he had some friends and allies on the council each year.[122] But failing that there were other procedures. Demosthenes tells us how Timocrates ought legally to have proceeded in order to secure the passage of his bill to allow bail to State debtors. In this particular case special leave to introduce the motion was required from the people. This done, he should have followed the usual course by making a written application (πρόσοδον γράφεσθαι) to the council and then (if they put the matter on the agenda) making a proposal in the assembly.[123] The right of 'application' was often granted to foreigners, and was apparently an inherent right of citizens.[124] Aeschines describes how Demosthenes used it —'he walked into the council chamber and pushing aside the ordinary members carried out a probouleuma to the assembly, exploiting the inexperience of the mover; and he got this motion put to the vote in the assembly too, and a decree of the people passed, when the assembly had already risen and I had left (or I never would have allowed it) and the majority had dispersed'.[125] How widely the right of 'application' was used we do not know. The council of course was not compelled to take the matter up,[126] and may well have killed large numbers of frivolous motions at birth; but it is unlikely that they would have refused to put on the agenda a proposal from anyone of political importance.

The inscriptions reveal the last resort of a private citizen who had some cause greatly at heart. In a number of cases a citizen moves in the assembly "that the council pass a probouleuma and bring it forward to the people that . . .". This might be done, as in the case of the ten generals, when the assembly already had the matter on its agenda, and wished to have it reintroduced at a later session.[127] But it would appear that this procedure could be used to introduce a topic *de novo*. Most cases are grants of honours,[128] but one is an important matter of public interest, Hegesippus' decree of 357-6, enacting the death penalty and confiscation of goods for anyone who molested the allies of Athens, which arose out of an attack on Eretria, but was of general application.[129] It seems likely that motions of this type might be made at the second assembly of each prytany, 'in which anyone who wishes may, having made a humble petition, speak to the people on any matter he wishes, private or public'.[130]

It would appear then that the control of the council over the assembly amounted to very little. It was no doubt the intention of the Athenians that the council, consisting of men of mature years and—in theory at any rate—of some substance, who were on oath and liable to prosecution if they betrayed their trust, should act as some check on possibly irresponsible conduct by the assembly. It was their duty to refuse to put to the vote illegal proposals, and they could refuse to give facilities to foolish ones. They no doubt saved the people's time by doing so, and by drafting uncontentious, but sometimes complicated, measures for the assembly's approval. Finally they saw to it that no motion was proposed without due notice and publicity. But policy was decided in the assembly.

What has been said above applies to decrees. For laws a more elaborate procedure was laid down in the fourth century at any rate. According to Aeschines it was the duty of the six thesmothetae, the judicial members of the college of archons, to make an annual review of the laws, and if they found any contradictions or ambiguities in the code, to post the relevant laws up. The presidents then held a special legislative session of the assembly, and the people voted which law to delete or to confirm.[131] It was presumably at this annual review that amendments could be made to the code under the procedure described by Demosthenes. On the eleventh day of the first prytany the code was submitted to a vote of the people section by section, the laws relating to the council, the general laws, those relating to the nine archons and to the other magistrates. If the people approved any section it stood. If they disapproved, the chairmen of the third assembly after this placed on its agenda the holding of a legislative meeting: meanwhile any citizen might post up new laws (with the old laws which they would supersede). The legislative assembly consisted of a limited number of citizens—in one case 1,001 plus the council of 500—from those who had taken the heliastic oath, and were therefore over 30. Having heard both the proposers of the new laws and five elected advocates for the old laws, it decided by vote.[132]

A procedure of this kind is first recorded when the laws were revised after the restoration of the democracy in 403,[133] and it probably did not exist before then. In the fifth century, at any rate, a number of enactments were passed as decrees which would have required legislation in the fourth, such as the establishment c. 448 of a priestess of Athena Nike and the allocation to her of a salary from public funds,[134] or the establishment in 434 of the treasurers of the other Gods, and the enactment of rules on the use of sacred funds.[135] These decrees were moved by ordinary

citizens. The regulations for the cult of Eleusis were drafted
c. 418 by a special board of draftsmen (συγγραφεῖς), but were
presented to the council and people by the normal procedure,
and amended in the assembly.[136] The appointment of a board of
draftsmen was not peculiar to changes of law; such a board
drafted regulations for Miletus,[137] and was no doubt appointed for
difficult and technical measures of any kind. What literary evidence we have suggests that the Athenians in the fifth century
were not acutely conscious of any such clear distinction between
laws and decrees as the orators of the fourth century insist upon
so strongly.[138] And finally, until the laws were codified between
411 and 403, it is difficult to see what mechanical test there can
have been to distinguish them from decrees.[139] The fourth-
century system may have had merits as ensuring the constitutional stability so much valued by the Greeks, but it made the
administration unduly rigid. No change, however minute,
could be made in the administrative routine except by legislation
on the one annual occasion set apart for it: even Peisitheides'
pension could only be put on a permanent basis by this process.[140]

A law passed by the proper procedure was still liable to be
quashed by the courts by the indictment of its author for passing
an inexpedient law, or one contradictory to a law still in the
code.[141] Decrees which were irregularly enacted, or whose
content conflicted with any law, were liable to the indictment
for illegal proceedings, which goes back to before 415[142]—
probably to 461[143]—though how exactly it was applied in the
absence of any clear distinction between laws and decrees is
obscure. This brings us to the vital part played in Athenian
politics by the courts. Not only could measures and their authors
be thus indicted, but many forms of indictment and impeach-
ment were available against politicians—for treason, deceiving the
people, peculation, bribery and so forth, and all were freely used.
The juries, which varied in size according to the importance of
the case, but in political cases normally numbered some thousands,[144] were chosen by lot from a panel, also chosen by lot, of

6,000 citizens.[145] All citizens, however poor, were eligible for this service,[146] and in the fifth century it would appear from Aristophanes' *Wasps* that the courts were mainly manned by old men of the humbler classes, who thus earned a meagre pension, or at any rate pocket money.[147] By Demosthenes' day the juries seem to have become predominantly middle or upper class. They probably acted as a conservative brake on the constitution—as for instance in quashing Hypereides' decree to free the slaves after Chaeronea.[148]

It would seem on the face of it that policy was initiated by any citizen who chose to offer his advice to the people, and was decided by the people in the assembly. Did the Athenians really guide their affairs as wisely as they did by this anarchic method, or was there some form of government, in the modern sense, official or unofficial, or were there parties, approximating to modern political parties, which provided alternative governments, or at the least supported coherent alternative policies? It is sometimes stated or implied that the ten generals formed a kind of government in the fifth century, and that they enjoyed certain constitutional prerogatives which helped them to perform this function.

The evidence for any important constitutional prerogatives is exceedingly weak. The generals were primarily executive officers in the military and naval spheres, and their duties were to mobilise armies and fleets on the instructions of the assembly, and to command such armies and fleets with a view to achieving objectives laid down, in more or less detail, by the people. They might, like other magistrates, or envoys, or the council, be given full powers, but, so far as we know, only within certain terms of reference. Thus Nicias, Alcibiades and Lamachus were given full powers 'to aid the Egestaeans against the Selinuntines, and to assist in the resettlement of Leontini, and to take such other action in Sicily as they should consider in the best interests of Athens': later they were given full power 'to act as they thought best about the size of the force and the whole expedition'.[149]

Occasionally, when secrecy was essential, as in the attempted seizure of Megara and the double attack on Boeotia in 424, the generals seem to have acted on their own initiative without consulting the people.[150]

It seems that the generals could be granted by the people, and normally were granted in wartime, priority of access to the presidents of the council and assembly, and perhaps the right of initiating business in the council and assembly. In one wartime decree the generals are instructed, with the presidents, to call an assembly,[151] and in another, it would seem, to initiate certain business.[152] In the second case a decree was as a result passed on the motion of the generals, and there is one other instance of this formula being used.[153] In another wartime decree certain business is given precedence before the council 'unless the generals require anything'.[154]

Such modest prerogatives hardly raised the generals above the level of the ordinary citizen, who could make an application to the council. In the fourth century generals seem normally to have followed this procedure; two decrees, moved in the normal way by a councillor in the council, begin 'with reference to the statement made by Timotheus the general' and 'whereas Timotheus the general states that . . .'.[155]

The idea that the board of generals acted as such as a government is manifestly false. The generals were ten individuals, who often advocated diametrically opposed policies, as did Nicias and Alcibiades over the Sicilian expedition. The utmost that can be said is that the people usually followed the advice of a general or generals, or that generals were usually political leaders and vice versa. This was partly because a general who had served many times had the necessary experience and technical knowledge to offer informed advice: thus when the Sicilian expedition had been decided upon, much against his will, an appeal was made to Nicias to estimate the forces required.[156] But it was even more due to the fact that in the fifth century the people elected as generals men whose opinion they respected, mainly on the rather irrelevant grounds of ancestry and wealth. This clearly comes out at the beginning of Alcibiades' career. 'Though still young at that date by the standard of any other city', says Thucydides, 'he was honoured for the distinction of his ancestors'. Annoyed by the Spartans having made their first unofficial approaches through two generals, Nicias and Laches, instead of through himself, though he had put himself out to look after their prisoners, he successfully persuaded the assembly to reject their pleas for a rapprochement, and was elected general (for the first time) next year.[157]

Anything like a continuous government was only achieved when one man (or a coherent group of men) succeeded in holding the confidence of the people over a long period, in which case he (or they) was usually in the fifth century regularly re-elected general. The most famous case is, of course, that of Pericles. There is no sound evidence that Pericles enjoyed any constitutional precedence over his colleagues, or indeed any special powers. This has been inferred from the fact that on two occasions, the Samian war of 440 and the first invasion of Attica in 431, Thucydides speaks of Pericles as commanding 'himself the tenth'.[158] But on the analogy of 'himself the fifth' and 'himself the third', which merely mean with four or two colleagues, this phrase was probably intended to emphasize that the importance of the operation was such that all ten generals served. And even if Thucydides did mean to convey by the phrase that Pericles was given some authority or precedence over his colleagues, he implies that such supreme authority was accorded to him specially for these particular operations, and not as a general rule.

It has also been inferred from the fact that, although normally the ten generals came each from a tribe, in several years (441, 439, 433, 432 and perhaps 431) two generals came from Pericles' tribe and none from another, that Pericles was chosen from the whole citizen body (as commander-in-chief). But in later years, when Pericles was dead, two generals were sometimes (probably in 426, and certainly in either 415 or 414) chosen from one tribe, and neither of the pair was a man on whom there was any reason to confer a supreme command.[159] The tribal rule was probably broken in order to give a chance to other able men in a tribe which possessed an outstanding general who was continually re-elected. We know too little of Athenian elections to understand how it was done. Candidates were as today nominated— usually it would seem in the assembly, though a formal probouleuma was required for elections as for any other business—and a vote taken between them, if more than one nomination was made.[160] It is possible that Aristotle's phrase 'one from each tribe' is inaccurate, and that what happened was that each tribe nominated candidates, between whom the whole people voted. In that case it would not have been impossible to arrange for a tribe which had no very distinguished candidate in its own number to select an outsider.[161]

An extraordinary constitutional position has also been inferred for Pericles from the fact that during the first invasion of Attica in 431 he 'did not hold an assembly or any meeting' of the Athenians.[162] But this refers to a state of emergency. During the actual invasion period, when all citizens were mobilised, the people may well have suspended sessions of the assembly, and have left it to the discretion of the generals (whose decisions would in fact be determined by Pericles, either in virtue of his personal prestige, or perhaps his authority as 'tenth himself') to summon an assembly or other meeting if they required it.

Pericles did not rule Athens for many years in virtue of any constitutional prerogatives. He owed his power, as Thucydides tells us, to his authority and judgment, and to his manifest incorruptibility.[163] He had to persuade the people to vote for every measure that he wished to have passed, and if they lost confidence in him they could, as they once did, depose and fine him,[164] and they could flout his advice, as again they did in trying to parley with the Spartans in 430.[165]

In the last third of the fifth century we find a new type of political leader emerging, an orator like Cleon, whom no one thought of electing general until he accidentally proved his ability. This became normal in the fourth century, when most generals carried little political weight, and the assembly was swayed by orators. The reason was no doubt the growing specialisation both in politics and in war. A gentleman of birth and wealth was no longer felt to be qualified as such both to advise the people and to take command in war. The army and navy were led by semi-professional generals like Iphicrates or Chabrias—in one case a foreign mercenary captain, Charidemus, was given the citizenship so that he might qualify—who also hired their services to other powers. They were thus much abroad and not in close touch with Athenian politics, and their loyalty was not above question. The other generals were mere lay figures. As Demosthenes complains: 'You elect from among yourselves ten regimental commanders, ten generals, ten squadron leaders and two cavalry commanders. Except for one, whom you send out to war, the rest organise processions with the managers of the festivals. You are like makers of terracotta statuettes: you make regimental commanders and squadron leaders for the market, not for war'.[166]

On the other hand politics, with the development of rhetorical technique, required special training. Many of the orators were men of family and wealth like Lycurgus, but it was possible for a poor man, like Aeschines or Demades, or indeed Demosthenes, whose inherited fortune was largely embezzled by his guardians, to achieve prominence. Being a politician must have been a full-time job, involving not only regular attendance at the assembly, but maintaining a watch on the council and keeping oneself informed on foreign affairs, finance, the navy, the corn supply and public affairs generally. Poor politicians seem generally to have maintained themselves at first by writing speeches for private litigants; Demosthenes did so, and Demades prided himself that he had not.[167] Having once gained a name they lived on politics. This did not necessarily mean, as Demosthenes alleged of his adversaries, that they were systematically bribed by foreign powers. Many no doubt did accept regular subsidies from foreign powers whose interests they supported on other grounds. More usually they seem to have accepted fees rather than bribes from interested parties, whether cities or individuals, who wished measures to be promoted in their favour.

The receipt of such payments was tolerated by public opinion. 'As I said in the assembly, members of the jury', declared Hypereides, 'you willingly allow generals and orators to make large profits—it is not the laws that allow them to do so, but your kindness and humanity—only maintaining one condition, that the money is taken for and not against your interests'. The profits were indeed large if Hypereides was correct in saying that 'Demosthenes and Demades had received more than 60 talents each just for decrees in the city and grants of honours to individuals, apart from the King's money, and Alexander's'.[168]

In the latter half of the fourth century certain important financial offices were made elective,[169] and the holders of these exercised great political influence. Thus Eubulus was one of the managers of the theoric fund,[170] into which surplus revenues flowed in peace time, and Lycurgus held an office concerned with the administration of the public revenues.[171] It is fairly certain however that these posts carried no constitutional prerogatives beyond some power of supervision over the minor financial officials: thus the Sellers farmed the taxes and mines 'with the treasurer of the military fund and those elected to manage the theoric fund'.[172] Aeschines, indeed, declares that 'owing to the confidence that you had in Eubulus, those elected to manage the theoric fund held the office of Auditor, and that of Receivers, and that of the Superintendents of the Dockyards, and built an arsenal, and acted as highway commissioners and had practically the whole administration of the city in their hands'.[173] But this is mere rhetoric. The position of the elective financial magistrates was probably similar to that of the generals in the fifth century. The people elected to these offices men whom it trusted, and by holding them they acquired experience which added to their authority. This appears clearly in the case of Lycur-gus, who held office for one quadrennium only (the post being quadrennial and re-election prohibited), but *de facto* administered the finances for twelve years.[174]

There was throughout Athenian history a class of semi-pro-fessional politicians, at first consisting of the gentry, later partly of the gentry and partly of poor men of rhetorical talent. These were the people who held the elective offices, were chosen as envoys to foreign States, proposed motions in the council and in the assembly, and prosecuted (and defended) in political trials. In the fourth century orators they are clearly recognised as a class, distinct from the mass of ordinary citizens, who held the offices which went by lot and merely voted in the council, assembly and law courts. The commoner apparently regarded the politicians with some suspicion, and Demosthenes in several passages exploits this feeling. 'In the old days, when the people dared to act and fight itself it was master of the politicians, and controlled all rewards, and it was a privilege for anyone to receive honour and office and rewards from the people. But today on the contrary the politicians control rewards, and everything is done through them, and you, the people . . . have become underlings, a mere appanage, content if they give you a share of the theoric moneys, or celebrate the Boedromia.'[175] Or again: 'If you acquit, the council will be in the hands of the orators: if you condemn, in those of the ordinary members. For when the majority see that this council has been deprived of its crown owing to the misconduct of the orators, they will not leave the business to them, but will give the best advice them-selves.'[176] Another speech in the Demosthenic corpus is full of abuse of politicians. 'But I do not imagine that their excuses and accusations and pretended feuds deceive you. For you have often seen them declaring that they are enemies in the courts and on the tribune and privately co-operating and sharing the profits.'[177]

There were no parties in anything like the modern sense,

either among the politicians or the general public. At the one end
of the scale there were groups or cliques among the politicians.
Demosthenes complains (the allusion is to the financial organisa-
tion of the war tax):[178] 'You conduct politics by symmories.
An orator is the director, and there is a general under him, and
the three hundred to cheer'.[179] But such alliances were probably
based on personalities rather than principles, and seem to have
been temporary.[180]

At the other end of scale there was a broad distinction of outlook between the propertied classes and the poor. Aristotle
thought that he could discern this distinction throughout Athenian political history,[181] and he is not likely to have been entirely
wrong. In domestic affairs it is difficult to trace it. There was
no overt oligarchical party. Oligarchs had to confine themselves
in normal times to cabals and intrigues and pamphlets, and only
came into the open when they could stage a counter-revolution,
as in 411, or had the armed backing of a foreign conqueror as in
404 and 322. All politicians had at any rate to pay lip service
to the democracy and oligarch was not even used as a term of
political abuse: in his most violent speech Demosthenes no more
than hints that Meidias and his friends are secret oligarchs.[182]

The distinction can be most clearly discerned in foreign policy—
which of course involved finance. On a number of occasions
we are told that the propertied classes favoured peace or appeasement, while the poor were more bellicose. The Oxyrhynchus
historian states that this was so in 396,[183] Diodorus on Alexander's
death.[184] Aristophanes declares: 'We must launch the fleet: the
poor man agrees, the rich and the farmers don't agree.'[185] But
this merely means that people tended to vote according to their
economic interests. The rich disliked paying war tax and serving
frequently as trierarchs, farmers feared their land would be rav-
aged and they themselves called up for military service. The poor
on the other hand had less to lose, and might hope for land allotments abroad in case of success, besides being more keenly
interested in the defence of the democratic régime, which they

rightly felt was threatened by the predominance of Sparta and Macedon.

The conclusion seems inevitable that Athenian policy was really determined by mass meetings of the citizens on the advice of anyone who could win the people's ear. The success of Athens is a testimony to the basic sense of the ordinary Athenian citizen. The assembly was, like all crowds, sometimes unduly swayed by mass emotion—anger as in the first debate on Mitylene, indignation as in the vote on the ten generals, or optimism as in the debates on the Sicilian expedition. In the first case it luckily recovered its judgment in time, and by a judicious breach of its standing orders reversed its decision. In the second it repented too late to save its victims. But in general the assembly seems to have kept its head, and very rarely to have broken its rules of procedure—the case of the ten generals would not have achieved such notoriety if such incidents had not been very rare.

Moreover the people demanded high standards of its advisers. Legally the proposer of a decree was responsible to the people; he could be—and frequently was—indicted if his motion was illegal or even if his policy was inexpedient. According to an ancient law cited by Deinarchus a 'speaker', in the technical sense of the proposer of a motion, had, like the generals, to own land in Attica and to have legitimate children,[186] and even if this law was a dead letter, it illustrates the serious view which the Athenians took of the responsibility attaching to political leadership.

In practice the people did not suffer fools gladly. Socrates remarks that in discussing any technical problem the people would listen only to experts, and booed and shouted down a clever speaker who wasted its time by ill-informed rhetoric.[187] Another anecdote told of Socrates illustrates the demands made by the assembly of its advisers.[188] Young Glaucon was ambitious to become a leading politician and kept making speeches, only to be howled down and make himself ridiculous. Socrates to wean him from his folly puts him through a little questionnaire. 'Tell me the sources of the revenues of the city at the present time, and their amount.' Glaucon confesses ignorance. 'Well, if you have omitted that question, tell us the expenses of the city: for obviously you are planning to cut down superfluous expenditure.' Glaucon can give no answer, and Socrates goes on. 'Then tell us first the military and naval strength of the city and secondly that of its enemies.' Glaucon again confesses ignorance. 'But I know that you have taken an interest in the security of the country, and know which garrisons are well placed and which not, and how many men are adequate or not.' Glaucon has never visited the frontier. 'I know you have not been to the silver mines, so as to know why they produce less than they used to do. But I am sure that you have not neglected the question of how long home-grown corn can feed the city, and how much extra is required annually.' It was informed advice, and not mere eloquence, that the people expected from rising politicians, and they saw to it that they got it.

NOTES

I. THE ECONOMIC BASIS OF THE ATHENIAN DEMOCRACY

[1] For the convenience of readers unfamiliar with Attic currency, the following table is given:

1 talent=60 minae=6,000 drachmae
1 mina = 100 drachmae
1 drachma=6 obols

Owing to the very different standards of living and patterns of spending it is useless and even misleading to try to translate Attic into modern currency, especially now when the value of money is changing so fast. The following facts will give a rough idea of the value of money in fifth- and fourth-century Athens (fourth-century prices and wages were higher than fifth.) In the Erechtheium accounts (*IG* I.² 373-4) of 409/8-407/6 B.C. the standard wage (for citizens, metics and slaves alike) is 1 drachma per day, occasionally 1½ drachmae. In the Eleusinian accounts (*IG* II-III.² 1672-3) of 329/8 and 327/6 B.C. unskilled labourers get 1½ drachmae per day, skilled men 2 or 2½ drachmae. In 351 B.C. Demosthenes (IV. 28) reckons 2 obols a day as ration allowance for soldiers and sailors: as he is trying to prove that his projected standing force can be cheaply maintained he is probably being optimistic. In the Eleusinian accounts public slaves are allowed 3 obols a day for food, and ephebes (young men of 18 and 19 undergoing military training) in the 330's were allowed 4 obols a day for their rations (Arist. *Ath. Pol.* 42. 3). Clothing was relatively dear. Tunics bought for the Eleusinian public slaves cost over 7 drachmae each, leather jerkins 4½, 3 or 2½, and shoes 6 drachmae a pair; a cloak is priced in Aristophanes' *Plutus*, 982-3 (of 388 B.C.) at 20 drachmae, and shoes at 8 drachmae—perhaps rather high prices in the context. For the maintenance of two girls and a boy, with a male nurse and a maid, in about 400 B.C. Lysias (XXXII. 28) allows 1,000 drachmae a year and Demosthenes (XXVII. 36), speaking in 363 B.C., accepts 700 drachmae a year as a reasonable sum for the maintenance of himself and his sister and mother during his minority. These work out at about 3⅓ obols and nearly 4 obols each per day, which seems very little, but rent is not included and Greeks considered that women and children ate much less than men. Disabled citizens who could do no work and owned less than 3 minae were given public assistance at the rate of 1 obol a day in the early fourth century and 2 obols in the late fourth (Arist. *Ath. Pol.* 49. 4, Lysias, XXIV. 13), but this was merely a dole; Lysias' client did follow a trade.

[2] Aristotle (*Ath. Pol.* 7. 4) commenting on Solon's exclusion of thetes from all offices, remarks: διὸ καὶ νῦν ἐπειδὰν ἔρηται τὸν μέλλοντα κληροῦσθαί τιν' ἀρχήν, ποῖον τέλος τελεῖ, οὐδ' ἂν εἷς εἴποι θητικόν. This seems to imply that

the Solonian rule was still technically in force, but ignored in practice. Similarly with the higher qualification for the Treasurers of Athena: κληροῦται δ' εἰς ἐκ τῆς φυλῆς ἐκ πεντακοσιομεδίμνων κατὰ τὸν Σόλωνος νόμον (ἔτι γὰρ ὁ νόμος κύριός ἐστιν), ἄρχει δ' ὁ λαχὼν κᾶν πάνυ πένης ᾖ (Arist. Ath. Pol. 47. 1). The 'Old Oligarch' declares that in his day (c. 425 B.C.) the δῆμος (which in his political terminology means roughly the thetes) filled the offices appointed by lot ([Xen.] Ath. Pol. i. 3).

³ Actually Pericles is only recorded to have introduced pay for jurors (Arist. Ath. Pol. 27. 3), but this was presumably the last stage in the process. Plato (Gorgias, 515e) attributes pay in general to Pericles.

⁴ For pay for office in general see [Xen.] Ath. Pol. i. 3, Thuc. VIII. 67. 3, Arist. Ath. Pol. 24. 3, 29. 5. Aristotle gives a few specific rates in Ath. Pol. 62. 2 (4 obols for the nine archons, a drachma for sundry other offices; cf. also 42. 3). Aristophanes (Ach. 66, 90) suggests that ambassadors received 2 drachmae (but Westermann in Class. Phil. 1910, pp. 203-16 infers about 1½ drachmae from inscriptions; this would include travelling expenses) and also that taxiarchs were paid, apparently 3 drachmae (id. ib. 595-607; cf. Larsen, Class. Phil. 1946, pp. 91-8), contrary to the general view (based on a misinterpretation of [Xen.] Ath. Pol. i. 3) that the elective military offices were unpaid.

⁵ Arist. Ath. Pol. 62. 2. It might be inferred from 29. 5 that the fifth-century rate was 3 obols, but a decree which abolished all pay except for a few essential offices may have reduced the rates for these.

⁶ Arist. Ath. Pol. 27. 3, 62. 2, Schol. on Aristoph. Wasps, 88, 300. The τριώβολον is first mentioned in the Knights (51, 255, etc.) of 424 B.C.

⁷ Arist. Ath. Pol. 41. 3. It appears from Aristoph. Eccl. 183-8, 380-93 (cf. 289-310) that only a limited number who arrived first got the pay, and that it was already (393-1 B.C.) 3 obols.

⁸ Arist. Ath. Pol. 62. 2.

⁹ The number 350 is based on a count from Arist. Ath. Pol. 47-61, which is a fairly exhaustive list (compare Gilbert, Greek Const. Ant. pp. 230-65, Busolt-Swoboda, Griechische Staatskunde, II, pp. 1081-1150). Our information for the fifth century is very incomplete, but known cases of old offices abolished and new offices created about cancel out. Arist. Ath. Pol. 24. 3, ἀρχαὶ δ' ἔνδημοι μὲν εἰς ἑπτακοσίους ἄνδρας, ὑπερόριοι δ' εἰς ἑπτακοσίους, is certainly corrupt on linguistic grounds, apart from being statistically impossible; perhaps the author gave 350 as the total for each class, making a total of 700. For rates of pay see note 4. A drachma seems on our limited evidence fairly universal, and if some got more, others got less, and some it appears only perquisites (e.g. the athlothetae, according to Arist. Ath. Pol. 62. 2, dined at public expense during the month in which the Panathenaea was held).

¹⁰ The council was summoned ὅσαι ἡμέραι πλὴν ἐάν τις ἀφέσιμος ᾖ (Arist. Ath. Pol. 43. 3: the excepted days would include festivals and assembly days, leaving perhaps 300). For irregular attendance see Dem. XXII. 36. Thuc. VIII. 69. 4, ἐπέστησαν τοῖς ἀπὸ τοῦ κυάμου βουλευταῖς οὖσιν ἐν τῷ βουλευτηρίῳ καὶ εἶπον αὐτοῖς ἐξιέναι λαβοῦσι τὸν μισθόν. ἔφερον δ' αὐτοῖς

τοῦ ὑπολοίπου χρόνου παντὸς αὐτοὶ καὶ ἐξιοῦσιν ἐδίδοσαν, has been taken to imply that councillors received a daily wage irrespective of attendance, but it is equally possible (and indeed suggested by the emphatic παντός) that the oligarchs gave the councillors the maximum they could have earned to get them to go quietly. Evidently members were paid day by day (since they were already paid up to date) and it is difficult to believe that in these circumstances they could claim for days when they were absent or no session was held.

[11] *Wasps*, 661–3.

[12] Dem. XXIV. 80.

[13] [Xen.] *Ath. Pol.* iii. 7.

[14] *Wasps*, 100 ff., 216 ff., etc.

[15] The figure is obtained by deducting 600 talents given by Thuc. II. 13. 3 as the gross revenue from the empire, from at least 1,000 talents given by Xenophon (*Anab.* VII. 1. 27) as the combined home and imperial revenue (both refer to the beginning of the Peloponnesian war). This is roughly confirmed by Aristophanes (*Wasps*, 656–60), who gives nearly 2,000 talents as the total revenue from all sources when the imperial tribute had been raised to 1,460 talents on paper (see *Ath. Trib. Lists*, III, pp. 344 ff.).

[16] Dem. X. 37.

[17] For this distinction see Dem. XXIV. 96–101.

[18] Lysias, XIX. 11, XXVII. 1, XXX. 22, Dem. XXIV. 96–101.

[19] Dem. X. 38, Theopompus, *FGH* II. 115, fr. 166.

[20] [Xen.] *Ath. Pol.* i. 16–8.

[21] Thuc. II. 13. 3 gives 600 talents, but the quota lists show a yield of only about 400 talents from the tribute of the allies (see *Ath. Trib. Lists*, III, pp. 333 ff.).

[22] E.g. in 446 B.C. after the suppression of the Euboean revolt all the inhabitants of Hestiaea were expelled and replaced by an Athenian colony (Thuc. I. 114. 3), while at Chalcis the aristocracy only were expropriated in favour of Athenian cleruchs (Aelian, *Var. Hist.* VI. 1, Plut. *Pericles*, 23).

[23] See Appendix.

[24] Plut. *Pericles*, 11.

[25] Thuc. II. 13. 8.

[26] Arist. *Ath. Pol.* 24. 3.

[27] Thuc. III. 17. 4, VI. 8. 1, 31. 3. After the Sicilian disaster the rate had to be cut to 3 obols owing to lack of funds (Thuc. VIII. 45. 2).

[28] See Tod, I. 53, and R. S. Stanier, *JHS* LXXXIII (1953), 68–76.

[29] Plut. *Pericles*, 12.

[30] Thuc. II. 13. 3, Tod, I. 64.

[31] Herod. VIII. 44.

[32] Herod. VIII. 1.

[33] Herod. IX. 28.

[34] Nepos, *Miltiades*, 5. Suidas, s.v. Ἱππίας (citing Ephorus).

[35] Herod. V. 97, VIII. 65. Aristophanes (*Eccl.* 1133) also gives this figure, though by this time (393–1) it was probably no longer true; he also (*Wasps*, 709) speaks of δύο μυριάδες τῶν δημοτικῶν (i.e. thetes) in 422.

³⁶ See Appendix.
³⁷ Thuc. I. 121. 3, 143. 1, VII. 13. 2, 63-4.
³⁸ Plut. *Pericles*, 11.
³⁹ Arist. *Ath: Pol.* 24. 3, Thuc. II. 13. 8.
⁴⁰ Thuc. IV. 101. 2.
⁴¹ id. V. 11. 2.
⁴² id. VI. 43, VII. 16. 2, 20. 2, 42. 1.
⁴³ id. III. 87. 3.
⁴⁴ Lysias, XX. 13, *ὑμῶν ψηφισαμένων πεντακισχιλίοις παραδοῦναι τὰ πράγματα καταλογεὺς ὧν ἐννακισχιλίους κατέλεξεν*: cf. Thuc. VIII. 97. 1, *τοῖς πεντακισχιλίοις ἐψηφίσαντο τὰ πράγματα παραδοῦναι (εἶναι δ' αὐτῶν ὁπόσοι καὶ ὅπλα παρέχονται)*. See Appendix.
⁴⁵ See pp. 76, 79, 81-2.
⁴⁶ See Gilbert, *Greek Const. Ant.* pp. 176-83, Busolt-Swoboda, *Griech. Staatskunde*, II, pp. 984-6. The minor role played by the merchant class in Athenian politics is explained partly because so many merchants were metics, partly because merchants were mostly humble folk, owning little more than their one ship, and operating on capital borrowed on its security and that of their cargo.
⁴⁷ Xen. *Mem.* II. viii. 1-5.
⁴⁸ Isaeus, V. 39, *εἰς δὲ τοὺς μισθωτοὺς ἰόντας δι' ἔνδειαν τῶν ἐπιτηδείων*, Isocr. XIV. 48, *ἄλλους δ' ἐπὶ θητείαν ἰόντας, τοὺς δ' ὅπως ἕκαστοι δύνανται τὰ καθ' ἡμέραν ποριζομένους*.
⁴⁹ Xen. *Mem.* II. v. 2, Dem. XXXVI. 28-9, 43.
⁵⁰ Plato, *Rep.* 565a.
⁵¹ Xen. *Mem.* III. vii. 6.
⁵² Arist. *Pol.* IV. iv. 21 (1291b).
⁵³ Lysias, V. 5. Cf. Dem. XLV. 86.
⁵⁴ E.g. the poor citizen, Chremylus, who is the hero of the *Plutus*, has a stock comic slave, Carion. In the *Ecclesiazusae* no slaves appear in the earlier part of the play when the women steal their husbands' clothes and the husbands subsequently wake up and have to put on their wives' clothes, but at the end a slave girl of Praxagora suddenly appears to do a comic turn. Yet Praxagora's communist programme includes *μηδ' ἀνδραπόδοις τὸν μὲν χρῆσθαι πολλοῖς, τὸν δ' οὐδ' ἀκολούθῳ* and she surely belongs to the second class.
⁵⁵ Thuc. III. 17. 4.
⁵⁶ Thuc. VII. 75. 5 implies that most of the attendants of the Athenian cavalry-men and hoplites at Syracuse were slaves.
⁵⁷ Thuc. IV. 101. 2. In Isaeus, V. 11, Dicaeogenes is reproached for sending a poor relation, whom he has defrauded of his inheritance, to serve his brother *ἀντ' ἀκολούθου* at Corinth (probably in the Corinthian war).
⁵⁸ Dem. XXIV. 197, *θύρας ἀφαιρεῖν καὶ στρώμαθ' ὑποσπᾶν καὶ διάκονον, εἴ τις ἐχρῆτο, ταύτην ἐνεχυράζειν*.
⁵⁹ See pp. 28-9.
⁶⁰ See pp. 88-9.
⁶¹ Lysias, VII. 9-10, Isaeus, XI. 42. The metics who are described as *γεωργοί*

in Tod, II. 100, are probably tenant farmers (they could not be owners of land), though they might be agricultural labourers. Cf. Xen. *Symp.* VIII. 25, on bad farming by tenants.

⁶² Lysias, IV. 1, VII. 16, 34, Dem. XLVII. 53, LIII. 6. The freedmen who describe themselves as γεωργοί in *IG* II–III.² 1553-78 (see Gomme, *Population of Athens*, pp. 41-3 for an analysis) were probably former agricultural slaves, now labourers or tenants. The ἄγροικος in Theophrastus (*Char.* IV. 5) discusses politics with his agricultural οἰκέται and μισθωτοί. An Athenian landowner in Naxos employed a πελάτης (apparently full time, ἐθήτευεν ἐκεῖ παρ᾽ ἡμῖν) as well as slaves (Plato, *Euthyphro*, 4c).

⁶³ Dem. LIII. 19-21.

⁶⁴ Dem. LVII. 45.

⁶⁵ Dem. XLVII. 52, Isaeus, VI. 33.

⁶⁶ Lysias, XX. 11.

⁶⁷ Dem. XXII. 65 = XXIV. 172, οἱ γεωργοῦντες καὶ φειδόμενοι, διὰ παιδοτροφίας δὲ καὶ οἰκεῖα ἀναλώματα καὶ λῃτουργίας ἑτέρας ἐκλελοιπότας εἰσφοράν. The liturgies here referred to cannot be the State liturgies, which fell on a relatively wealthy class, but those of the demes (Isaeus, II. 42, *IG* I². 186-7B, II-III². 1178, 1198, 1200).

⁶⁸ *Pol.* 1323a, cf. 1252b, ὁ γὰρ βοῦς ἀντ᾽ οἰκέτου τοῖς πένησίν ἐστιν.

⁶⁹ See pp. 83-4.

⁷⁰ Dem. XXI. 83, 95.

⁷¹ Lysias, XVI. 14.

⁷² For the price of land see below, p. 142, note 36. Rents are reckoned at about 8 per cent. of capital value in Isaeus, XI. 42 and *IG* II-III.² 2496. For the cost of living see note 1. The poor farmers in Aristophanes' *Plutus* (223-4) are represented as working in the fields themselves.

⁷³ Xen. *Vect.* iv. 14-15. Xenophon was writing over two generations later, quoting popular report, which may well have exaggerated Nicias' wealth (cf. Lysias, XIX. 47).

⁷⁴ Dem. XXXVII. 4.

⁷⁵ Lysias, XII. 19

⁷⁶ Dem. XXXVI. 11; Demosthenes' 32-3 knifemakers brought in half a talent a year (Dem. XXVII. 9). See Dem. XXXVI. 5, for Pasion's land.

⁷⁷ Dem. XXVII. 9-11.

⁷⁸ [Plut.] *Vit. X Or. Isocrates* (*Mor.* 836E).

⁷⁹ Xen. *Mem.* II. vii. 3-6.

⁸⁰ Xen. *Mem.* III. xi. 4.

⁸¹ Aesch. I. 97.

⁸² Lycurgus, *c. Leocr.* 23, 58; Demosthenes (XXVII. 9) reckons his skilled knifemakers at 3 minae a head at the lowest.

⁸³ Isaeus, VIII. 35.

⁸⁴ Isaeus, VI. 19, 20, 33-34.

⁸⁵ Xen. *Mem.* II. iii, 3, οἰκέτας μὲν οἱ δυνάμενοι ὠνοῦνται ἵνα συνέργους ἔχωσιν.

⁸⁶ Lysias, XXIV. 6, τέχνην δὲ κέκτημαι βραχέα δυναμένην ὠφελεῖν, ἣν αὐτὸς μὲν ἤδη χαλεπῶς ἐργάζομαι, τὸν διαδεξόμενον δ᾽ αὐτὴν οὔπω δύναμαι κτήσασθαι.

⁸⁷ Suidas, s.v. ἀποψηφίσεις (453 B).

⁸⁸ Ath. VI. 272c.

⁸⁹ Die Bevölkerung der griechisch-römischen Welt, pp. 84-99, cf. also R. L. Sargent, The size of the slave population at Athens during the fifth and fourth centuries B.C., and W. L. Westermann, 'Athenaeus and the slaves of Athens,' in Athenian Studies presented to W. S. Ferguson.

⁹⁰ Thuc. VII. 27. 5. The figure must be an estimate, but even Thucydides' estimates are worthy of serious consideration. He implies that this loss was a very serious matter for the Athenians, i.e. that 20,000 was a substantial proportion of the total slave population.

⁹¹ Xen. Vect. iv. 25.

⁹² Xen. Vect. iv. 22, πολλοὶ δ᾽ εἰσὶ καὶ αὐτῶν τῶν ἐν τοῖς ἔργοις γηράσκοντες, πολλοὶ δὲ καὶ ἄλλοι καὶ ᾽Αθηναῖοι καὶ ξένοι οἳ τῷ σώματι μὲν οὔτε βούλοιντ᾽ ἂν οὔτε δύναιντ᾽ ἂν ἐργάζεσθαι, τῇ δὲ γνώμῃ ἐπιμελούμενοι ἡδέως ἂν τὰ ἐπιτήδεια πορίζοιντο.

⁹³ Dem. XLII. 20, πολλὰ ἐκ τῶν ἔργων τῶν ἀργυρειων ἐγώ, Φαίνιππε, πρότερον αὐτὸς τῷ ἐμαυτοῦ σώματι πονῶν καὶ ἐργαζόμενος συνελεξάμην.

⁹⁴ Arist. Ath. Pol. 62. 3.

⁹⁵ Dem. XIII. 2, 10.

⁹⁶ Gilbert, Greek Const. Ant. pp. 173-4.

⁹⁷ op. cit. p. 229.

⁹⁸ Xen. Vect. iv. 25.

⁹⁹ The evidence is fully set out and analysed by Margaret Crosby in Hesperia, 1950, pp. 189 ff.

¹⁰⁰ Suidas, s.v. ἀγράφων μετάλλων δίκη.

¹⁰¹ Xen. Hell. I. vi. 24, Aristoph. Frogs, 693-4.

¹⁰² Arist. Ath. Pol. 40. 2.

¹⁰³ [Plut.] Vit. X Or. Hypereides (Mor. 849A).

¹⁰⁴ [Xen.] Ath. Pol. i. 10.

¹⁰⁵ Xen. Hell. II. iii. 48.

¹⁰⁶ Plato, Rep. 563b.

II. THE ATHENS OF DEMOSTHENES

¹ II. 62. 7.

² XIV. 19, 27; cf. Philochorus, FGH III. 328. fr. 46.

³ XXVII. 9.

⁴ Pollux, VIII. 130.

⁵ JG II-III². 2496. Isaeus, XI. 42, assumes 8 per cent as a normal rent for land.

[6] E.g. Lysias, III. 24; Isaeus, VII. 39, XI. 47; Isocrates, VII. 35; Dem. XXVII. 8, XXVIII. 3-4, XLII. 22-3, XLV. 66; Aeschines, I. 101; cf. Plato, *Rep.* 343d.

[7] XXVII. 7, 9, XXVIII. 4, XXIX. 59.

[8] XXVII. 37.

[9] In his new edition of Bury's *History of Greece*, p. 890.

[10] E.g. Lysias, XIX. 28-30, 42-3.

[11] See now his article in *Classica et Mediaevalia*, XIV (1953), pp. 30-70.

[12] Dem. XXVIII. 4, cf. XXI. 157.

[13] See note 25.

[14] Dem. XXII. 44.

[15] Leptines ἐκ Κοίλης and Callicrates son of Eupherus, whom Demosthenes cites in XXII. 60, were trierarchs (*IG* II-III.[2] 1609, II, l. 72; cf. 1622c, ll. 361-3, 375-7, and 1622B, ll. 165-6).

[16] Dem. XXII. 60. I have assumed that this paragraph refers to the arrears which Androtion actually collected, seven talents according to XXII. 44. If the whole fourteen talents were in small sums the total of debtors would be about double.

[17] Isaeus, VI. 60, καὶ τὰς εἰσφορὰς εἰσενηνόχασιν ἀμφότεροι πάσας ἐν τοῖς τριακοσίοις ... εἰς δὲ τοὺς τριακοσίους ἐγγέγραπται καὶ εἰσφέρει τὰς εἰσφοράς.

[18] Cf. the incident recorded in Dem. III. 4-5.

[19] Dem. L. 8.

[20] See note 17.

[21] Dem. L. 9 shows that προεισφορά was a liturgy subject to the normal rules.

[22] This is implied by Dem. L. 8-9, προσεπηνέχθη μου τοὔνομα ἐν τριττυῖς δήμοις ... τούτων ἐγὼ ... ἔθηκα τὰς προεισφορὰς πρῶτος.

[23] Dem. L. 10.

[24] XXIV. 111; cf. I. 20, II. 31, where, addressing the assembly, he speaks loosely of everyone paying εἰσφορά.

[25] The evidence is Cleidemus (*FGH* III. 323, fr. 8) quoted by Photius, s.v. ναυκραρία: he speaks of 100 symmories, and these must be those of the εἰσφορά, since the trierarchic symmories numbered only 20 (Dem. XIV. 17). The figure is confirmed by the Three Hundred προεισφέροντες (Dem. XLII. 25); for the Three Hundred seem to be identical with τοὺς ἡγεμόνας τῶν συμμοριῶν ἢ τοὺς δευτέρους καὶ τρίτους (Dem. XVIII. 103; cf. Aesch. III. 222). We know from Dem. XXVIII. 4, XXI. 157 that the εἰσφορά symmories had ἡγεμόνες whereas the trierarchic had ἐπιμεληταί (Dem. XLVII. 21, 22, 24).

[26] Dem. XIV. 16-7.

[27] XXVII. 7, XXVIII. 4.

[28] XXIX. 59.

[29] Diod. XVIII. 18. 4-5.

[30] XXII. 44.

[31] XXVII. 37.

[32] Xen. *Hell.* VI. ii. 1.

³³ XIV. 27; cf. III. 4 for a war tax of 60 talents (1 per cent.) actually voted if not collected.

³⁴ XXII. 65 (=XXIV. 172), οἱ γεωργοῦντες καὶ φειδόμενοι δι: παιδοτροφίας δὲ καὶ οἰκεῖα ἀναλώματα καὶ λειτουργίας ἑτέρας ἐκλελοιπότες εἰσφοράς. This is not to say that all who owed arrears of εἰσφορά were poor men. Cf. note 15.

³⁵ Dem. XLII. 22.

³⁶ Lysias, XIX. 29, 42. Aristophanes bought more than 300 *plethra* of land and a house (of the value of 50 minae) for rather more than 5 talents. The price works out at about 85 drachmae the *plethron*, or about 360 drachmae the acre.

³⁷ Cf. note 5.

³⁸ Cf. note 86.

³⁹ XV. 107-13.

⁴⁰ Dem. XLIX. 6-21.

⁴¹ Xen. *Hell.* VI. ii. 37.

⁴² *Ib.* VI. v. 49; Diod. XV. 84. 2, XVI. 37. 3, 85. 2, XVIII. 10. 2, 11. 3.

⁴³ IV. 21.

⁴⁴ IV. 28-9.

⁴⁵ Arist. *Ath. Pol.* 42. 3.

⁴⁶ The Eleusis accounts of 329 B.C. (*IG* II-III². 1672, ll. 4-5, 42-3, 117-18 141-2).

⁴⁷ XIX. 84, ἡ πρότερον βοήθει᾽ εἰς Πύλας ... ἦν μετὰ πλειόνων ἢ διακοσίων ταλάντων ἐποιήσασθε, ἂν λογίσησθε τὰς ἰδίας δαπάνας τάς τῶν στρατευσαμένων.

⁴⁸ I. 27, εἰ γὰρ ὑμᾶς δεήσειεν αὐτοὺς τριάκονθ᾽ ἡμέρας μόνας ἔξω γενέσθαι, καὶ ὅσ᾽ ἀνάγκη στρατοπέδῳ χρωμένους τῶν ἐκ τῆς χώρας λαμβάνειν, μηδενὸς ὄντος ἐν αὐτῇ πολεμίου λέγω, πλείον᾽ ἂν οἶμαι ζημιωθῆναι τοὺς γεωργοῦντας ὑμῶν ἢ ὅσ᾽ εἰς ἅπαντα τὸν πρὸ τοῦ πόλεμον δεδαπάνησθε.

⁴⁹ Thuc. III. 17. 4.

⁵⁰ It appears from Harpocration, s.v. θῆτες (citing Aristophanes), that θῆτες did not serve as hoplites; cf. Thuc. III. 16. 1, VI. 43, VIII. 24. 2. The Solonian classes were by the fourth century based on property, not income (Isaeus, VII. 39). The figure of 2,000 drachmae for zeugites is an inference from Diod. XVIII. 18. 4-5, on the assumption that Antipater set up a hoplite franchise. The figure was probably reached by multiplying by ten the Solonian income of 200 μέτρα (Arist. *Ath. Pol.* 7. 4), converted on the Solonian scale of values (Plut. *Solon*, 23) into 200 drachmae; this figure is slightly confirmed by the value of the Lesbian κλῆροι (Thuc. III. 50. 2) which were probably intended to raise thetic occupants to zeugite status.

⁵¹ XXI. 83, 95.

⁵² Lysias, XVI. 14.

⁵³ Isocr. VIII. 48; Dem. XXI. 154-5 (cf. L. 6-7, 16, III. 4, IV. 36).

⁵⁴ That this was the rate till the Sicilian disaster (when it was halved, Thuc. VIII. 45. 3) is shown by Thuc. III. 17. 4, VI. 31. 3; cf. VI. 8. 1 (a trireme costs a talent a month).

⁵⁵ Dem. L. 10, 12, 14, 23, 53.
⁵⁶ *Ib.* 11-12.
⁵⁷ XLIX. 11-12.
⁵⁸ L. 17, 56.
⁵⁹ XLVII. 21, 44.
⁶⁰ XXI. 154-5, XVIII. 102-4.
⁶¹ XIV. 16-20. It should be observed that the trierarchic symmories are under this scheme to provide σώματα (persons to act as trierarchs), but that the expense is to fall on the whole τίμημα τῆς χώρας of 6,000 talents.
⁶² Dem. XVIII. 102-4; Aesch. III. 222; Harpocration, s.v. συμμορία, (citing Hypereides).
⁶³ Dem. XIII. 2, τἀργύριον μέν ἐστι τοῦθ', ὑπὲρ οὗ βουλεύεσθε, μικρόν, τὸ δ' ἔθος μέγα, ὃ γίγνεται μετὰ τούτου.
⁶⁴ LIX. 4-5; for the meaning of διοίκησις see XXIV. 96-101.
⁶⁵ I. 19-20, XIII. 2, 10; cf. III. 10-13, 19, 31, Harpocration, s.v. θεωρικά, Suidas, s.v. θεωρικά, θεωρικόν, Libanius, *Hypoth. in Olynth.* I. 4.
⁶⁶ X. 38.
⁶⁷ See p. 76.
⁶⁸ Hesychius, s.v. δραχμὴ χαλαζῶσα; cf. Harpocration, s.v. θεωρικά.
⁶⁹ Hesychius, s.v. θεωρικὰ χρήματα.
⁷⁰ I. 26.
⁷¹ *Mor.* 818E F.
⁷² [Plut.] *Vit. X Or. Lycurgus (Mor.* 843D).
⁷³ Dem. X. 35-43.
⁷⁴ Plut. *Mor.* 1011B.
⁷⁵ Dem. XIX. 291.
⁷⁶ Dem. XXI. 203.
⁷⁷ X. 35 ff., esp. 39.
⁷⁸ XVIII. 10, cf. *Hell. Oxy.* i. 2-3, and Aristophanes, *Eccl.* 197-8, for a similar situation in the early fourth century.
⁷⁹ E.g. I. 6, 20, II. 24, 27, 31, III. 33, IV. 7, VIII. 23, X. 19.
⁸⁰ XIV. 27.
⁸¹ XXI. 83, 95. Cf. the very apologetic and humble tone taken to the jury by a really poor litigant in LVII. esp. 25, 31, 35, 45.
⁸² XXII. 47 ff., XXIV. 160 ff., esp. 197.
⁸³ He merely says airily that there will always be enough men to perform the liturgies (XX. 22), a statement refuted by XXI. 13. [Xen.] *Ath. Pol.* i. 13, emphasises how the δῆμος draws money from the choregi and gymnasiarchs ᾄδων καὶ τρέχων καὶ ὀρχούμενος.
⁸⁴ Leptines' law opened with the preamble ὅπως ἂν οἱ πλουσιώτατοι λητουργῶσιν (XX. 127), and his argument, which Demosthenes tries to refute, was ὡς αἱ λειτουργίαι νῦν μὲν εἰς πένητας ἀνθρώπους ἔρχονται, ἐκ δὲ τοῦ νόμου τούτου λητουργήσουσιν οἱ πλουσιώτατοι (XX. 18).
⁸⁵ Deinarchus, *in Dem.* 42.
⁸⁶ In the Eleusinian accounts (*IG* II-III.² 1672) of 329 B.C., 3 obols is allowed

for τροφή for the public slaves (ll. 4-5, 42-3, 117-18, 141-2); casual labourers (μισθωτοί) doing unskilled work get 1½ drachmae (ll. 28-30, 32-4, 45-6, 60-2); skilled men get 2 drachmae (ll. 110-11, carpenters, 177-8, stone polishers) or 2½ drachmae (26-8, bricklayers, 31-2, stone masons).

III. THE ATHENIAN DEMOCRACY AND ITS CRITICS

[1] The latter part of this paper, dealing with Thucydides, owes much to, and is indeed in parts a summary of, an article by my former pupil, Mr. G. E. M. de Ste Croix, entitled 'The character of the Athenian Empire', since published in *Historia* III (1954-5), pp. 1-41. I owe Mr. de Ste Croix a deep debt of gratitude for having allowed me to anticipate his article (where the questions at issue are more fully discussed and documented), and also for many comments, criticisms and references in the earlier part of my paper, which he read in MS. I also wish to express my gratitude to Mr. A. G. Woodhead, who read this paper in MS. and offered a number of useful comments.

[2] I have not, save for occasional references, included Aristophanes—or, for that matter, the tragedians—in my survey, because with Gomme (*Class. Rev.* LII (1938), pp. 97-107) I hold that Aristophanes wrote comedies and not political tracts. While he makes it fairly obvious that he strongly disliked certain features of the democracy, such as vulgar politicians like Cleon, he does not—and did not intend to—preach political doctrine, and his jokes cannot necessarily be taken for criticism.

[3] *Pol.* V. ix. 15 (1310a).

[4] *Pol.* VI. ii. 3 (1317b); iv. 20 (1319b).

[5] VII. 37; cf. VII. 20, XII. 131.

[6] VIII. 557b.

[7] *Ib.* 563b. The same complaint about metics and slaves is made in [Xen.] *Ath. Pol.* i. 10-12.

[8] See Dem. XXI. 46-50 and IX. 3 on slaves.

[9] Thuc. II. 37. 2. Cf. Nicias' words, τῆς ἐν αὐτῇ ἀνεπιτάκτου πᾶσιν ἐς τὴν δίαιταν ἐξουσίας (*id.* VII. 69. 2).

[10] Cf. Eurip. *Hippolytus*, 421-3; *Ion*, 670-2.

[11] XX. 106.

[12] *Mem.* I. ii. 12 ff.; cf. Aesch. I. 173.

[13] *Republic*, VIII. 558c; cf. *Laws*, VI. 757.

[14] VII. 21; cf. III. 14.

[15] *Pol.* II. ix. 1-5 (1280a); V. i. 2-7 (1301a); VI. ii. 2 (1317b). In VI. iii (1318a) Aristotle makes an ingenious attempt to combine democratic and oligarchic equality.

[16] For praise of ἰσότης see Eurip. *Supplices*, 404-8, 433-41; *Phoenissae*, 535ff.

[17] XXI. 67.

¹⁸ XXIV. 59.

¹⁹ Thuc. II. 37. 1.

²⁰ Xen. *Hell.* II. iii. 51.

²¹ *Pol.* III. xi. 1–2 (1281b); in §5 he limits this argument to certain bodies of men only, excluding those in which the majority are 'brutes'.

²² *Pol.* III. xi. 14 (1282a); here again he limits the argument to cases where the majority are not 'too slavish'.

²³ *Protagoras*, 319b–323a.

²⁴ Xen. *Mem.* I. ii. 9.

²⁵ XXXIX. 10–11.

²⁶ Arist. *Ath. Pol.* 55. 2; cf. Lysias, XVI and XXXI, for hostile speeches at a δοκιμασία.

²⁷ *Ib.* 43. 4.

²⁸ *Ib.* 48. 3–5, 54. 2.

²⁹ Thuc. II. 37. 1.

³⁰ Plato, *Menex.* 238cd.

³¹ Arist. *Pol.* II. xii. 2 (1273b).

³² For the fourth century see J. Sundwall, 'Epigraphische Beiträge', *Klio*, Beiheft IV (1906), §§2, 5, 8.

³³ [Xen.] *Ath. Pol.* i. 3.

³⁴ *Mem.* III. iv. 1.

³⁵ XIX. 237. In 282 Demosthenes states what he thinks are the proper qualifications for high office—trierarchies, liturgies, etc. Cf. the vulgar abuse of Cleon and other politicians as being low persons engaged in trade by Aristophanes in the *Knights*.

³⁶ Aristophanes jibes at ambassadors with their 2 drachmae a day (*Acharnians*, 66, 90) and military officers with 3 drachmae (*ib.* 595–607).

³⁷ *Pol.* IV. vi. 5–6 (1293a); elsewhere Aristotle is prepared to accept political pay, provided that precautions are taken to prevent the poor outnumbering the rich (IV. xiii. 6 (1297a), xiv. 13 (1298b)).

³⁸ See above, pp. 35–7.

³⁹ Lysias, XIII. 20. Rich men like Demosthenes and Apollodorus apparently found no difficulty in securing a seat on the council when convenient (Dem. XXI. 111; XIX. 154, 286; LIX. 3–4). See also J. Sundwall, *op. cit.* §1 (pp. 1–18).

⁴⁰ *Gorgias*, 515e.

⁴¹ Arist. *Ath. Pol.* 62. 3.

⁴² *Ib.* 43. 3.

⁴³ See above, p. 143, note 86.

⁴⁴ VII. 54; VIII. 130. But see n. 38.

⁴⁵ *Pol.* IV. iv. 25 (1292a); vi. 2–6 (1292b–93a).

⁴⁶ *Mem.* IV. iv. 13–14.

⁴⁷ *Mem.* I. ii. 40–6.

⁴⁸ XXIV. 76.

⁴⁹ Andoc. I. 81–5.

⁵⁰ As in Tod, I. 74; Arist. *Ath. Pol.* 29. 2.

⁵¹ This appears from the fact that the commissioners of 411 thought it necessary to repeal the γραφὴ παρανόμων (and other similar constitutional safeguards) before any substantive change of the law was proposed (Arist. *Ath. Pol.* 29. 4; Thuc. VIII. 67. 2).

⁵² Dem. XX. 88 ff.; XXIV. 18 ff.; Aesch. III. 38 ff.

⁵³ Dem. XX. 91; Aesch. III. 3.

⁵⁴ Dem. LIX. 4.

⁵⁵ Aesch. III. 194.

⁵⁶ Dem. LIX. 5.

⁵⁷ I. 4, repeated verbatim in III. 6.

⁵⁸ XXIV. 5.

⁵⁹ XXIV. 75-6.

⁶⁰ *C. Leocr.* 4.

⁶¹ III. 5.

⁶² *Hell.* I. vii.

⁶³ *Ib.* II. iv. 43. Cf. Plato, *Menex.* 243e, *Epist.* vii, 325b, and Isocr. XVIII. 31-2, 44, 46, 68.

⁶⁴ [Xen.] *Ath. Pol.* i. 4-9.

⁶⁵ VIII. 557a.

⁶⁶ *Pol.* III. vii. 5 (1279b); viii. 2-7 (1279b-80a); IV. iv. 1-3, 6 (1290ab).

⁶⁷ VI. 39. 1.

⁶⁸ Cf. [Xen.] *Ath. Pol.* i. 3; Dem. XXIV. 112; Arist. *Ath. Pol.* 21. 1; Eupolis, fr. 117. Cf. note 32.

⁶⁹ J. Sundwall, *op. cit.* §8 (pp. 59-84).

⁷⁰ VIII. 128.

⁷¹ XV. 159-60.

⁷² See above, pp. 29-32.

⁷³ Cf. Xen. *Mem.* III. iv. 3; Dem. XIX. 282.

⁷⁴ XXI. 1-5.

⁷⁵ Dem. XX. 8 shows that a man could claim a year's exemption after a liturgy: if there were, as Demosthenes says (XXI. 21), only about sixty liturgies to fill per annum, they cannot have fallen very often on the individual rich citizen.

⁷⁶ XXI. 156 (cf. 154).

⁷⁷ Isaeus, V. 35-6.

⁷⁸ Lysias' client reckons 6 talents for seven years (XXI. 2); Demosthenes states that a contractor would take over a trierarchy for 1 talent (XXI. 155), but himself paid only 20 minae (a third of a talent) in lieu of performing a (half?) trierarchy (XXI. 80). In Lysias, XIX. 29 and 42, the speaker claims to have spent 80 minae (1⅓ talents) on three (half?) trierarchies.

⁷⁹ Isaeus, VII. 32, 42.

⁸⁰ Isocr. XVIII. 59-60; Lysias, XXXII. 24; Dem. L. 39, 68.

⁸¹ Dem. XLVII. 21, 44; cf. XIV. 16-17.

⁸² Lysias, XXI. 2. He could have claimed two years' exemption after each year of service (Isaeus, VII. 38).

⁸³ Lysias, XIX. 29, 42-3.

[84] Isocr. XV. 145.

[85] Lysias, XIX. 57-9.

[86] *Ib.* 63.

[87] Dem. XXVII. 7-9; cf. XXVIII. 11; XXIX. 59.

[88] Dem. XVIII. 102-4; XXI. 154-5.

[89] Isocr. XV. 160; cf. Plato, *Rep.* VIII. 565a; Arist. *Pol.* V. v. 1, 5 (1304b-1305a); VI. v. 3, 5 (1320a).

[90] Sycophants are fully dealt with in R. J. Bonner and G. Smith, *The Administration of Justice from Homer to Aristotle*, II, Chapter iii, and J. O. Lofberg, *Sycophancy in Athens* (Chicago, 1917).

[91] Arist. *Ath. Pol.* 35. 4; Xen. *Hell.* II. iii. 21; Lysias, XII. 5 ff.

[92] Plut. *Mor.* 843 D.

[93] XXX. 22; XXVII. 1; XIX. 11. There is a similar suggestion in Aristophanes, *Knights*, 1358-61.

[94] X. 44-5.

[95] III. 33-6.

[96] Ἀρχὴ ἄνδρα δείξει seems to be a democratic proverb; it is attributed to Bias of Priene by Aristotle (*Ethica Nicomachea*, V. i. 16) and quoted by Demosthenes (*proem* 48).

[97] II. 18-19.

[98] II. 65. 7-11.

[99] Apart from the unfavourable notices in III. 36. 6 and IV. 21. 3 there is a note of spite in IV. 28. 5 and 39. 3 and especially in V. 16. 1.

[100] Dem. XL. 25.

[101] I. 98. 4.

[102] Thucydides' use of the word δουλόω is discussed in *The Athenian Tribute Lists*, III. pp. 155-7.

[103] V. 85-113.

[104] III. 37-40 (esp. 37. 2).

[105] II. 63.

[106] I. 75-7.

[107] VI. 82-7 (esp. 85. 1).

[108] I. 22. 1.

[109] [Lysias], II. 55-7; Isocr. IV. 100-9, 117-20; XII. 54, 59-61, 68.

[110] 242a-243a.

[111] II. 8. 4-5; VIII. 2. 1-2.

[112] III. 47. 2.

[113] III. 27.

[114] IV. 84-8.

[115] IV. 110-13, 123. 1-2, 130. 2-7.

[116] VIII. 9. 2-3, 14. 1-2.

[117] VIII. 44. 1-2.

[118] VIII. 21, 72; Xen. *Hell.* II. ii. 6; iii. 6; Tod, I. 96; II. 97.

[119] Herod. IX. 35. 2; cf. Andrewes in *Phoenix*, VI (1952), 1-5, for the chronology.

¹²⁰ Thuc. V. 81. 1. It is worth noting that the Mantineans before the battle speak of their anticipated position if they lost it (and became allies of Sparta again) as δουλεία (Thuc. V. 69. 1).

¹²¹ Xen. *Hell*. III. ii. 21ff.

¹²² Incidentally Sparta took hostages from her Arcadian allies to ensure their loyalty (Thuc. V. 61. 5).

¹²³ Thuc. I. 139. 3, 144. 2.

¹²⁴ For Athens the evidence is collected in G. F. Hill, *Sources for Greek History* (edd. Meiggs and Andrewes, 1951), p. 355, and in *The Athenian Tribute Lists*, III. pp. 149–54. Sparta sometimes installed or tightened oligarchies without any pretext, as at Argos and Sicyon (Thuc. V. 81. 2).

¹²⁵ I. 97. 1.

¹²⁶ I. 141. 6–7.

¹²⁷ III. 10–12, esp. 10. 4–5 and 11. 3–4. The chronology is studiously vague, but the Mitylenaeans are referring to a period after 449 (when Athens had 'relaxed her hostility to the Persians') and indeed to a time when the only allies on the congress still supplying ships were Chios and Lesbos, that is 440 at the earliest. The Mitylenaeans would scarcely be at such pains to excuse their submissiveness to Athens in voting for war against rebel allies unless they had done so recently in a famous case.

¹²⁸ I. 121. 1.

¹²⁹ The Spartans later had a guilty conscience about this (Thuc. VII. 18. 2).

¹³⁰ As in 440, when Corinth persuaded the Peloponnesian congress not to make war on Athens (Thuc. I. 40. 5). The initiative in this earlier proposal to violate the Thirty Years' Peace must have come from Sparta, since she alone could summon a league congress, and naturally only did so when she approved the proposal to be debated.

¹³¹ Samos herself had seventy ships in 440 (Thuc. I. 116. 1), and Lesbos and Chios provided forty-five to assist Athens against her (I. 116. 2, 117. 2). This was far from their full strength, for Chios in 411, after losses in the Sicilian expedition (VI. 43; VII. 20. 2), had sixty ships left (VIII. 6. 4).

¹³² As the 'Old Oligarch' explains ([Xen.] *Ath. Pol.* i. 14–16). For an Athenian defence of the system see Thuc. I. 77; Isocrates, IV. 113; XII. 60.

¹³³ The clause in the alliance between Sparta and Athens, ἢν δὲ ἡ δουλεία ἐπανιστῆται ἐπικουρεῖν Ἀθηναίους Λακεδαιμονίοις, appears to have been standard, seeing that Sparta was able to call up all her allies in the great revolt of 464 (Thuc. I. 102. 1; cf. II. 27. 2 for Aegina, III. 54. 5 for Plataea and Xen. *Hell.* V. ii. 3 for Mantinea.

¹³⁴ III 36. 4.

¹³⁵ This emerges from Tod, I. 62. The subscriptions were evidently collected by the Spartan admiral Alcidas (see F. E. Adcock, 'Alcidas ἀργυρολόγος' in *Mélanges Glotz*, I. 1-6) who seems to have called twice at Melos, on his way out and on his way back—hence the two Melian subscriptions recorded.

¹³⁶ Thuc. III. 91. 1-2.

¹³⁷ Thuc. III. 52. 4, 68. 1-2.

[138] The phrase is used in *Pol.* III. iv. 12 (1277b); IV. xii. 3 (1296b); IV. xiv. 7 (1298a); V. x. 30, 35 (1312b); V. xi. 11 (1313b); VI. v. 5 (1320a). From the first three passages it appears that Aristotle considered a democracy 'extreme' when working people are in a majority and can hold office, and the people is sovereign.

IV. THE SOCIAL STRUCTURE OF ATHENS IN THE FOURTH CENTURY B.C.

[1] Athenaeus, VI. 272C.

[2] Dem. XXV. 51.

[3] Plut. *Phocion*, 28. 7; Diod. XVIII. 18. 5. One may add that according to [Plut.] *Vit. X Or. Lycurgus* (*Mor.* 843 D) the confiscated property of Diphilus, worth 160 talents, was distributed between the citizens at 50, or as others say, 100 drachmae each—yielding the result of 19,000 + on the 50 drachmae basis. I do not understand Gomme's argument (*The Population of Athens*, p. 18) that 'it is the latter (Diodorus') figure only which is consistent with the statistics of the Lamian war discussed above'. Diodorus' figures for the Lamian war (see below, notes 26–7) refer to hoplites only.

[4] 453B, s.v. ἀποψηφίσεις.

[5] *IG* II–III.² 1672, discussed by Gomme, op. cit. pp. 28 ff. and A. Jardé, *Les céréales dans l'antiquité grecque*, pp. 36 ff.

[6] Jardé, op. cit. pp. 123–4, 130–1.

[7] In the absence of any census of animals certainty is impossible, but on Jardé's very conservative estimates (op. cit. pp. 124–7) more than the whole crop would be required for animal feed.

[8] Dem. XX. 31–2.

[9] Jardé, op. cit. pp. 128 ff.

[10] Thuc. VII. 27. 5.

[11] Xen. *Vect.* iv. 25.

[12] See above, p. 142, note 50.

[13] Dem. III. 4.

[14] See above, p. 142, note 6.

[15] Lysias, XXXIV, *hypothesis*.

[16] Rather similar conditions prevail in some countries today. If I may quote from personal experience, my domestic servant Abdu in Cairo owned (jointly with a brother, I believe) a very small holding including some shares in some date palms in Abu Simbel, where he kept his wife and children. Abdu earned most of his income in wages in Cairo, but spent a third of the year at home.

[17] Dem. XXVII. 9, reckons his knife-makers as worth 5 or 6 or at a minimum 3 minae.

[18] Isaeus, V. 39 and Isocr. XIV. 48, speak of μισθωτοί or those who go ἐπὶ θήτειαν as being the lowest of the low. For wages see above, p. 143, note 86.

¹⁹ For details on State pay see above, p. 136, notes 4–14; for the social standing of βουλευταί, p. 145, note 39.

²⁰ *IG* II–III.² 1672, lines 4–5, 42–3, 117–18, 141–2 (rations) 102–5, 190, 230, (clothes and shoes).

²¹ See above, pp. 36–7.

²² Arist. *Ath. Pol.* 62. 2.

²³ See above, pp. 33–5.

²⁴ Lysias, XX. 13; cf. Thuc. VIII. 97. 1.

²⁵ The Athenians put 6,600 men into the field in 394 (Xen. *Hell.* IV. ii. 17), 6,000 in 362 (Diod. XV. 84), 5,400 in 352 (Diod. XVI. 37).

²⁶ Diod. XVIII. 10. 2, 11. 3, gives 5,000 hoplites and 500 cavalry from seven out of the ten tribes.

²⁷ Xen. *Vect.* ii. 2–5, is explicit that metics normally served on expeditions and were not reserved as they were in 431 (Thuc. II. 13. 7) for garrison duty. Diodorus (loc. cit.) distinguishes πολιτικοί from μισθόφοροι in the Athenian forces in the Lamian War; metics would clearly fall in the former category.

²⁸ *IG* II–III.² 1156, gives 43–5 ephebes for Cecropis in 334–3; *Hesperia, Suppl.* VIII, 273, gives 53–5 for Oeneis *c.* 330, *Ephemeris Archaiologike*, 1918, 73 gives 63 for Leontis in 327–6. There is also a later figure (*IG* II–III.² 478) of about 33 ephebes for Erechtheis in 305–4, which must be multiplied by twelve, as there were by then twelve tribes. See Gomme, *op. cit.* pp. 67–70 for these figures.

²⁹ *IG* II–III.² 1926. Mr. D. M. Lewis has reconstructed part of another list of arbitrators (*BSA* L (1955), 27–36). This gives not less than fifty-four names for the first five tribes.

³⁰ *Past and Present*, IV (1953), pp. 1–31.

³¹ See diagram.

³² Dem. XXI. 83, 95.

³³ Lysias, XVI. 14.

³⁴ See above, p. 141, note 25.

³⁵ Dem. XIV. 16–17.

³⁶ Dem. XXVII. 7; XXVIII. 4; cf. XXIX. 59.

³⁷ Dem. XXII. 65 (=XXIV. 172).

³⁸ Dem. XXIV. 197.

³⁹ See above, pp. 23ff.

⁴⁰ Isaeus, V. 35–6.

⁴¹ Isaeus, VII. 32, 42.

⁴² Isaeus, XI. 42 (5½ tal.); VII. 32, 42 (5 tal.); X. 23 (4 tal.+); XI. 44 (3 tal. 4000 dr.); VI. 33 (*c.* 3½ tal.); III. 2 (3 tal.); XI. 41 (2½ tal.); VIII. 35 (over 90 minae).

⁴³ Dem. XXVII. 64.

⁴⁴ Dem. XLII. 1–5, 25; see above, p. 141, note 25.

⁴⁵ Dem. XXVII. 7, 9; XXVIII. 4; XXIX. 59.

⁴⁶ Lysias, XIX. 45 ff.

⁴⁷ Lysias, XIX. 40.

⁴⁸ [Plut.] *Mor.* 843D.

⁴⁹ Hypereides, III. 35.
⁵⁰ Harpocration and Suidas, s.v. Ἐπικράτης.
⁵¹ Dem. XXXVI. 5 ff.
⁵² Dem. XVIII. 102-4; cf. XXI. 154-5.
⁵³ This is implied by Dem. XVIII. 103 (the opposition of the ἡγεμόνες, δεύτεροι and τρίτοι to the law; cf. Deinarchus, in Dem. 43) and Aesch. III. 223 (the number of trierarchs reduced to 300), and confirmed by Harpocration, s.v. συμμορία (citing Hypereides for 300 trierarchs divided into symmories of 15).
⁵⁴ Dem. XXXVI. 11.
⁵⁵ Lysias, XII. 19.
⁵⁶ Dem. XXVII. 9 ff.
⁵⁷ Dem. XLIX. 11.
⁵⁸ Dem. L. 8.
⁵⁹ Xen. Oec. passim, esp. xx. 22-9; for his fortune Lysias, XIX. 46.
⁶⁰ Dem. XLII. 5 (40 stades round), 7 (wood), 20 (barley and wine).
⁶¹ The following table sets out the facts:

Reference	Land (and stock)	House property	Industrial slaves	Money
Isaeus, V. 22	60 πλέθρα in the Plain	2 οἰκίδια and 1 βαλανεῖον	—	—
Isaeus, VI. 33	ἀγρός at Athmonia (75 minae), goats, goatherd and two teams (26½ minae)	οἰκία at Athens (mortgaged for 44 minae), βαλανεῖον in Serangium (30 minae). Also (ch. 19-20) a brothel in Peiraeus and a wine shop in Ceramcicus.	δημιουργοί	—
Isaeus, VIII. 35	ἀγρός at Phlya (1 tal.)	2 houses at Athens (20 and 13 minae)	ἀνδράποδα μισθοφοροῦντα (with 3 female slaves and furniture worth 13 minae)	—
Isaeus, XI. 41	ἀγρός at Eleusis (2 tal.). 60 sheep, 100 goats, 1 horse	—	—	—
Isaeus, XI. 42-3	ἀγρός at Thria (2½ tal.). Sheep, stock and crops (49 minae)	houses at Melite (30 minae) and Eleusis (5 minae)	—	loans (40 minae) ἔρανοι (10 minae) cash (9 minae)

| Isaeus,
XI. 44 | χωρία at Oenoe
and Prospalta (50
and 30 minae) | house at Athens
(20 minae) | —   — |
| Aesch.
I. 97 ff. | ἐσχατία at Sphet-
tos, χωρίον at
Alopece (20 minae).
His father had sold
a χωρίον at
Cephisia and an
ἄγρος at Amphi-
tropae (ch. 101) | house at Athens
(20 minae). His
father had sold
two ἐργαστήρια
in the mines (ch.
101). | 9 or 10 σκυτοτόμοι, loans
1 ποικιλτής,
and a woman
weaver |

[62] Xen. *Mem.* II. vii. 3-6.

[63] Xen. *Vect.* iv. 14-15 has to go back to the fifth century for examples.

[64] Xen. *Vect.* iv. and *Hesperia*, 1950, pp. 189 ff.; cf. Hopper, *BSA*, XLVIII (1953), pp. 200 ff.

[65] Xen. *Vect.* iv. 22.

[66] Dem. XLII. 20.

[67] Dem. XXXVII. 4.

[68] Hypereides, III. 36.

[69] This point is rightly emphasised by M. I. Finley, *Studies in Land and Credit in Ancient Athens 500-200 B.C.*, pp. 74 ff.

[70] Tod, II. 100.

[71] Dem. XLV. 63; XXXVI. 50.

[72] Besides Pasion and Phormio, Demosthenes mentions Socrates, Satyrus and Timodemus as freedmen bankers (XXXVI. 28-9) and Socles who bequeathed his widow to Timodemus cannot have been an Athenian. Eumathes (Isaeus *frag.* xii) and Epigenes and Conon (Deinarchus, I. 43) were metics. Nothing is known of Pylades (Dem. XXVII. 11), Heracleides (XXXIII. 6), Blepaeus (XL. 52) or Theocles (LIII. 9).

[73] Lysias, XXXII. 4, 6, 15, 25.

[74] Andoc. II. 11.

[75] In Dem. LII. 20 two brothers, Megacleides and Thrasyllus, of Eleusis, borrow for a voyage to Ace.

[76] Lampis was a metic (Dem. XXXIV. 37, οἰκῶν 'Αθήνησι), Hegestratus a Massaliot (XXXII. 5, 8), Apaturius a Byzantine (XXXIII. 6), Artemon a Phaselite (XXXV. 1-3, 15) Lycon a Heracleot (LII. 3) and his partner Cephisiades a metic (LII. 3, 9). Cf. *IG* II-III.² 360, 408.

[77] Dem. XXVII. 11. Other Athenian investors in bottomry are Diodotus (Lysias, XXXII. 6) and Androcles; but his partner Nausicrates is a Carystian (Dem. XXXV. 10). Foreign lenders include Theodore the Phoenician (XXXIV. 6), Lycon the Heracleot (LII. 20), and Chrysippus (as appears from XXXIV. 38, 50). Many of the lenders are themselves merchants or retired merchants (Lysias, XXXII. 4, 6; Dem. XXXIII. 4; XXXIV. 38; LII. 20).

[78] Besides Cephalus (Lysias, XII. 19) and Pasion (Dem. XXXVI. 11) another metic industrialist is Leocrates (Lycurgus, *c. Leocr.* 23. 58). Athenians include

Demosthenes' father (Dem. XXVII. 9 ff.), Isocrates' father (Plut. *Mor.* 836E), Comon (Dem. XLVIII. 12), Timarchus, Euctemon and Ciron (see note 61), and the three men mentioned in Xen. *Mem.* II. vii. 3–6. These are slave owners. Many humble Athenians worked as craftsmen themselves, as is shown by Xen. *Mem.* III. vii. 6 and Aristophanes, *Plutus*, 510 ff.

[79] [Dem.] XVII. 15.

[80] Xen. *Hell.* I. vi. 24; cf. Aristophanes, *Frogs*, 190, 693.

[81] [Plut.] *Mor.* 849A; cf. Lycurgus, *c. Leocr.* 41.

[82] Dem. XXXIV. 39.

[83] Xen. *Vect.* iii. 2.

[84] Dem. XXXIV. 37; XXXV. 50–1; cf. LVI. 5–6, 11, 13.

[85] Dem. XXXV. 10.

[86] Dem. XXXIV. 36; cf. XX. 29 ff. and Tod, II. 167.

[87] Xen. *Hipparchicus,* iv. 7.

[88] Xen. *Vect.* iv. 6.

[89] Xen. *Vect.* iii. 2.

[90] Thuc. IV. 108. 1.

V. HOW DID THE ATHENIAN DEMOCRACY WORK?

[1] Thuc. VI. 89. 6.

[2] Xen.*Mem.* III. iii. 8 ff., v. 16–21, *Hipparchicus,* i. 7 *et passim.*

[3] Xen. *Hipparchicus,* i. 19.

[4] Arist. *Ath. Pol.* 61. 4, 5.

[5] *Ib.* 49. Cf. Xen. op. cit. i. 8.

[6] [Xen.] *Ath. Pol.,* ii. 1 ff.

[7] Xen. *Mem.* III. v. esp. 21 ff.

[8] The taxiarchs appointed the λοχαγοί, Arist. *Ath. Pol.* 61. 3.

[9] Arist. *Ath. Pol.* 46. 1.

[10] Tod, I. 96, line 30 (νεωροί), II. 200, line 179 (ἐπιμεληταὶ τῶν νεωρίων); cf. Dem. XXII. 63, XLVII. 21, 26, Aesch. III. 25. Their accounts are published in *IG* II–III.[2] 1604–32; nos. 1607 and 1623 show that they were ten, one from each tribe.

[11] Tod, II. 200, lines 250–5, cf. Dem. XVIII. 107, XLVII. 26, L. 10.

[12] Gilbert, *Gr. Const. Ant.* 370–6, Busolt-Swoboda, *Gr. Staatskunde,* II. 1199 ff., *P.W.K.* VIIA, 106 ff.

[13] Dem. XXI. 80, 155, LI. 7 ff.

[14] Dem. LI. 1, Tod, II. 200, lines 189 ff.

[15] Thuc. VI. 31. 3, Dem. L. 7.

[16] Thuc. I. 143. 1, [Xen.] *Ath. Pol.* i. 2.

[17] Xen. *Mem.* III. iii. 12.

[18] The three principal archons managed the major festivals (Arist. *Ath. Pol.*

56. 3-5, 57. 1, 58. 1), assisted by boards of ἀθλοθέται, (chosen by lot) for the Panathenaea (op. cit. 60. 1), of ἐπιμεληταί (at first elected, later chosen by lot) for the Dionysia (op. cit. 56. 4, cf. Dem. XXI. 15, IV. 35) and of ἐπιμεληταί (elected) for the Mysteries (Arist. *Ath. Pol.* 57. 1, Dem. XXI. 171). There were also two boards of ἱεροποιοί, chosen by lot (Arist. *Ath. Pol.* 54. 6, 7).

19 Gilbert, *Gr. Const. Ant.*, 359-63, Busolt-Swoboda, *Gr. Staatskunde*, II, 1086 ff.

20 Xen. *Mem.* III. iv. 4.

21 Dem. XXI. 15, 17, 58-60, cf. [Xen.] *Ath. Pol.* i. 13.

22 See p. 129.

23 See above, pp. 23 ff.

24 Arist. *Ath. Pol.* 47. 1.

25 Tod, I. 51; for the suppression of the office see Busolt-Swoboda, *Gr. Staatskunde*, II. 1139.

26 For specimens of their accounts see Tod, I. 50, 55, 64, 69-70, 75, 78, 81, 83, 92.

27 Tod, I. 30, 51A, Arist. *Ath. Pol.* 54.

28 Op. cit., 48. 3.

29 This appears to be the distinction drawn in Dem. XXIV. 96 ff. between τὰ ἐκ τῶν τελῶν χρήματα and τὰ προσκαταβλήματα: cf. Aristoph. *Wasps*, 658-9.

30 Dem. XLIII. 71, LVIII. 48, Andoc. I. 77, 79. Aesch. I. 35, *Lex. Seguer.* 190. 26. There is incidentally no justification for the statement often made on the strength of Aristoph. *Knights*, 1358-61 and Lysias, XXVII. 1, that fines went directly to pay the jurors. It is clear from Dem. XXIV. 97-9 that the pay of jurors, as of the council and the assembly, came out of the same pool as the expenditure on the cavalry and the sacrifices.

31 Arist. *Ath. Pol.* 47. 2-3.

32 Op. cit., 47. 5, 48. 1-2, cf. Tod, II. 116, μερίσαι δὲ τὸ ἀργύριον τὸ εἰρημένον (in the decree) τοὺς ἀποδέκτας ἐκ τῶν καταβαλλομένων χρημάτων, ἐπειδὰν τὰ ἐκ τῶν νόμων μερ[ίσωσι].

33 Called τὰ κατὰ τὰ ψηφίσματα ἀναλισκόμενα or μεριζόμενα τῷ δήμῳ (e.g. Tod, II. 135, 142, 153, 167, 173, 178, 198) or τὰ δέκα τάλαντα (ib. 123, 139).

34 *IG* II-III². 120, lines 21-2.

35 *Syll.*³ 313.

36 Arist. *Ath. Pol.* 50. 1, 56. 4.

37 See notes 33 and 34.

38 Dem. XXII. 17: cf. the elected treasurers of the two sacred triremes, who had an annual allocation of 12 talents each (Arist. *Ath. Pol.* 61. 7, Dem. XXI. 171, 174).

39 Arist. *Ath. Pol.* 47. 3-4, Dem. XXIV. 98-9.

40 Lysias, XXX. 19-22.

41 Dem. XXIV. 99.

42 Dem. XXXIX. 17; cf. XLV. 4.

⁴³ Lysias, XXX. 22.

⁴⁴ Tod, I. 91 (=SEG X. 138): cf. II. 167, where the treasurer of the people is instructed to supply money for crowns from the assembly's fund, but for the present (presumably because the ten talents were exhausted) the Receivers are to pay it from the military fund.

⁴⁵ Syll.³ 226.

⁴⁶ Syll.³ 298.

⁴⁷ See above, p. 48.

⁴⁸ [Xen.] Ath. Pol. i. 3, Dem. XXIV. 112, cf. LVII. 25, Arist. Ath. Pol., 7. 4, 47. 1.

⁴⁹ Dem. LIX. 72 (Theogenes, a man of good family but poor, only enters for the office of basileus when a wealthy friend promises to help with his expenses on entering office and to serve as his assessor).

⁵⁰ Arist. Ath. Pol. 47. 5, 48. 1: the same man had custody of the archives (Dem. XIX. 129).

⁵¹ Arist. Ath. Pol. 55. 1–2.

⁵² Ib. 54. 3–5.

⁵³ Lysias, XXX. 2, 27–8.

⁵⁴ Dem. XVIII. 261, XIX. 70, 200, 249; also merely abusive references in XVIII. 127, 265, XIX. 95, 314.

⁵⁵ Lysias, XXX. 29.

⁵⁶ Arist. Ath. Pol. 47. 1.

⁵⁷ Arist. Ath. Pol. 45. 4, cf. Dem. XIX. 185, XXII. 5.

⁵⁸ Arist. Ath. Pol. 43. 2.

⁵⁹ Op. cit., 62. 1. For an analysis of deme representation see A. W. Gomme, The Population of Athens, Note A (pp. 49–66), J. A. O. Larsen, Representative Government in Greek and Roman History, 5–9.

⁶⁰ Xen. Mem. I. ii. 35.

⁶¹ Arist. Ath. Pol. 22. 2, cf. Xen. Mem. I. i. 18, Lysias, XXXI. 1, 2, Dem. XXIV. 147–8, LIX. 4.

⁶² Arist. Ath. Pol. 45. 3, cf. Dem. XXI. 111; Lysias XVI and XXXI were delivered at the dokimasia of a bouleutes.

⁶³ Aesch. III. 20, Dem. XXII. 38–9.

⁶⁴ Larsen, op. cit., 15–18.

⁶⁵ Arist. Ath. Pol. 62. 3.

⁶⁶ See above, p. 150, note 28.

⁶⁷ See above, p. 145, note 39.

⁶⁸ Aesch. III. 62, cf. 73.

⁶⁹ Arist. Ath. Pol. 62. 1. This practice of letting a carpet–bagger stand accounts for the slight variations in the number of councillors from each deme which the inscriptions show, see Larsen, op. cit., 7–8.

⁷⁰ Arist. Ath. Pol. 43. 2–3.

⁷¹ Op. cit., 44. 1–3: for the earlier system see besides the inscriptions the passages cited in notes 73–4 and the comic account of a council meeting in Aristoph. Knights, 624–82 (esp. 665, 674) and of an assembly in Acharnians, 19 ff. (esp. 23, 40).

⁷² Aesch. III. 3.
⁷³ Thuc. VI. 14.
⁷⁴ Xen. *Hell.* I. vii. 14-5, Plato, *Apol.* 32b. In Xen. *Mem.* I. i. 18, IV. iv. 2, Plato, *Gorg.* 473e Socrates is represented as being actually ἐπιστάτης, but the less dramatic version of the story is preferable.
⁷⁵ Aesch. II. 84.
⁷⁶ Dem. XXII. 36-7, cf. XXIV. 147 and Xen. *Hipparchicus*, i. 8 and Aesch. III. 9 for ῥήτορες in the council.
⁷⁷ Arist. *Ath. Pol.* 43. 4-6. cf. 30. 5 for the use of the lot in selecting agenda: the same rules on agenda applied in the council (Dem. XIX. 185).
⁷⁸ Aesch. II. 72.
⁷⁹ Thuc. VI. 8, Aesch. II. 65-67.
⁸⁰ Thuc. VIII. 72. 1.
⁸¹ Plut. *Arist.* 7, Philochorus, *FGH* III. 328. fr. 30.
⁸² Dem. LIX. 89.
⁸³ Dem. XXIV. 45-6.
⁸⁴ Aristoph. *Acharnians*, 21-2, *Eccles.* 378-9, and the scholiasts and lexicographers. It may be noted that in the Acharnians this device is employed for a κυρία ἐκκλησία (the first of the prytany), when the business was dull and formal; later extra pay was given for κυρίαι ἐκκλησίαι (Arist. *Ath. Pol.* 62. 2).
⁸⁵ Xen. *Mem.* III. vii. 6.
⁸⁶ See above, pp. 35-6.
⁸⁷ Dem. XIV, esp. 24 ff.
⁸⁸ Dem. XIX. 291.
⁸⁹ Dem. XVIII. 169-70.
⁹⁰ Lines 295-310, 331-51, 372-9. For other allusions to the prayer and curse see Dem. XVIII. 282, XIX. 70-1, XXIII. 97, Deinarchus I. 47-8, II. 17, and for the herald's invitation to speak Aesch. I. 23.
⁹¹ Tod, I. 31, 66, 84ʙ, 86, 96, II. 97.
⁹² As in I. 96 and II. 97.
⁹³ *Ib.* I. 84ʙ; cf. *BSA* XLVI (1951), p. 200 for a revised text and interpretation.
⁹⁴ *Ib.* I. 86.
⁹⁵ *Ib.* I. 44, 74.
⁹⁶ *Ib.* I. 42. The words αὐτίκα μάλα also occur in *SEG* X. 14, Tod, I. 61, 77, II, 114, 123, 142, 144, 146, *Syll.*³ 198, 204. In all these immediate action by or in the assembly is proposed, presumably in the assembly. When the words occur in a decree of the council they refer to action to be taken forthwith in or by council, as in Tod, II. 103 and *Syll.*³ 227, lines 18 and 30, and also Tod. II. 97 and 137, which appear to be probouleumata adopted *en bloc* by the assembly.
⁹⁷ *Ib.* I. 61.
⁹⁸ *Ib.* I. 84ʙ.
⁹⁹ E.g. in Tod. II. 114, 136, 174-5, 178, etc.
¹⁰⁰ In Tod. II. 123, 142, 144, 146, 147, 168, *IG* II-III.² 70, 134, although the prescript is ἔδοξε τῇ βουλῇ καὶ τῷ δήμῳ, the decree itself incorporates the words δεδόχθαι or ἐψηφίσθαι τῷ δήμῳ, which shows that (in the form in which it

was engraved) it was moved in the assembly. Furthermore 123 contains the clause ἑλέσθαι τὸν δῆμον πρέσβεις τρεῖς αὐτίκα μάλα: 142 has similarly ἀναγράψαι δὲ αὐτῶν τὰ ὀνόματα αὐτίκα μάλα ἐνάντιον τοῦ δήμου; and 144 and 146 open εὐξάσθαι μὲν τὸν κήρυκα αὐτίκα μάλα.

[101] Tod. II. 103 (alliance with Eretria) must have been confirmed by the people, and would not have been engraved until it was confirmed; yet it is headed ἔδοξε τῇ βουλῇ. It seems unlikely too that the honours voted by the council to Dionysius of Syracuse (ib. II. 108) were not ratified by the people. In IG II–III.[2] 32 a decree headed ἔδοξε τῇ βουλῇ is followed by an amendment τὰ μὲν ἄλλα κάθαπερ τῇ βουλῇ, and must therefore have been passed by the people.

[102] Tod, II. 134, 167, 181.

[103] Aesch. II. 64, 68.

[104] Tod, I. 90.

[105] Ib. II. 97A.

[106] E.g. in Tod, II. 124, 126, 131, 133, 135, 143, 157, 159, 170.

[107] Ib. II. 189.

[108] IG II–III.[2] 336.

[109] Tod, II. 144.

[110] Ib. II. 114.

[111] Ib. II. 118, 121, 123.

[112] Ib. II. 124, 126.

[113] Thuc. I. 31–44, 139–45, III. 36–49, IV. 17–22, V. 44–6, VI. 8–26. Cf. the debate on Pylos, in which Nicias resigned the generalship in favour of Cleon, in IV. 27–8.

[114] Xen. Hell. I. vii.

[115] Aesch. II. 65–68.

[116] Dem. LIX. 4. Cf. XXIII. 9, 14, for the tactical convenience of having a probouleuma ready for a snap vote.

[117] Dem. XXI. 162.

[118] Dem. LIX. 4.

[119] Dem. XIX. 286.

[120] Dem. XIX. 234 (cf. Aesch. II. 45–6), XVIII. 28 (cf. Aesch. II. 55), XVIII. 25, XIX. 154. Cf. also Aesch. II. 19.

[121] Dem. XIX. 31.

[122] Cf. Xenophon's advice to a hipparch ἐν τῇ βουλῇ ἔχειν ῥήτορας ἐπιτηδείους (Hipparchicus i. 8).

[123] Dem. XXIV. 48.

[124] E.g. Tod, II. 131, 133, 173 for foreigners. The clause in the decree of Tisamenus (Andoc. I. 84), ἐξεῖναι δὲ καὶ ἰδιώτῃ τῷ βουλομένῳ εἰσιόντι εἰς τὴν βουλὴν συμβουλεύειν ὅτι ἂν ἀγαθὸν ἔχῃ περὶ τῶν νόμων should, I think, be taken to mean that private citizens were on this occasion officially encouraged to use their rights. Cf. Andoc. I. 111, Dem. XIX. 10, 17, XXIV. 11, for προσιέναι τῇ βουλῇ. Decrees passed as a result of a πρόσοδος normally in the fourth century begin with some such words as περὶ ὧν λέγουσι . . . . In

most cases the persons alluded to are foreign envoys (e.g. Tod, II. 122, 124, 126, 131, 133-5, 146-7, 159, 167-8, 175, 178, 189) but sometimes citizens (*IG* II-III.² 70, 243 and probably Tod. II. 108), including priests (*IG* II-III². 47, 410) and other functionaries (*ib.* 403).

125 Aesch. III. 125-6.

126 This appears from the last clause of Tod. I. 74, ἡ δὲ βουλὴ ἐς τὸν δῆμον ἐχσενενκέτω ἐπάναγκες (the report of Lampon on the Eleusinian first-fruits of oil).

127 Xen. *Hell.* I. vii. 7.

128 *Syll.*³ 281 (a decree of the people beginning περὶ ὧν ὁ δῆμος προσέταξεν τῇ βουλῇ προβουλεύσασαν ἐξενειγκεῖν περὶ Πυθέου καθ᾽ὅτι τιμηθήσεται ὑπὸ τοῦ δήμου), 304 (which gives the whole procedure, IA the original motion in the people by Telemachus of Acharnae, IB the probouleuma moved by his fellow demesman Cephisodotus, and IC the final decree of the people moved by Telemachus: IIA is a second and later probouleuma, resulting in IIB a second decree).

129 Tod. II. 154 (here only the original motion in the people is recorded, and it is apparently assumed that the council and people duly confirmed it).

130 Arist. *Ath. Pol.* 43. 6.

131 Aesch. III. 38-40.

132 Dem. XXIV. 17 ff. cf. XX. 81 ff. For the number of the νομοθέται see Dem. XXIV. 27 (whence Pollux, VIII. 101): in Andoc. I. 84 they number 500 only (again plus the council), and are elected by the demes. Despite the heliastic oath (Dem. XXIV. 21) the νομοθέται followed the procedure of the assembly, and were presided over by πρόεδροι and an ἐπιστάτης (*Syll.*³ 200, 226, and *Hesperia* XXI (1952), p. 355).

133 Andoc. I. 81 ff. discussed by Harrison in *JHS* 1955, pp. 22 ff.

134 Tod. I. 40. Contrast the νομοθεσία required in the fourth century for an annual payment of 30 drachmae for a sacrifice to Amphiaraus (*Syll.*³ 298).

135 Tod. I. 51. Contrast the νομοθεσία required for altering the rules about the surplus (Dem. III. 10-11).

136 Tod. I. 74. Contrast legislation on the same topic in 353/2 (*Syll.*³ 200).

137 *SEG.* X. 14. The most famous board of συγγραφεῖς is of course that of 411 (Thuc. VIII. 67. 1, Arist. *Ath. Pol.* 29. 2).

138 See above, p. 51.

139 See Harrison, *JHS*, 1955, pp. 22 ff.

140 *Syll.*³ 226.

141 Dem. XXIV. 33.

142 Andoc. I. 17: it was evidently regarded as a bulwark of the constitution in 411, Thuc. VIII. 67. 2, Arist. *Ath. Pol.* 29. 4.

143 It was presumably one of the safeguards substituted in 461 for ἡ τῆς πολιτείας φυλακή of the Areopagus (Arist. *Ath. Pol.* 25. 2).

144 Dem. XXIV. 9 (1000), Deinarchus, *in Dem.* 109 (1,500), Lysias XIII. 35 (2,000), Deinarchus *in Dem.* 52 (2500). In Andoc. I. 17 the whole body of 6,000 jurors formed the jury, it would seem.

¹⁴⁵ Arist. *Ath. Pol.* 24. 3, Aristoph. *Wasps*, 661 (6,000); Arist. *Ath. Pol.* 27. 4 (the lot).

¹⁴⁶ Arist. *Ath. Pol.* 63. 3, cf. 7. 3.

¹⁴⁷ Aristoph. *Wasps*, 605 ff. for the fee: the jurors are represented as old men (χόρος γερόντων σφηκῶν, cf. *Knights* 255, ὦ γέροντες ἡλιάσται), and former rowers in the fleet (cf. *Wasps*, 231). The Old Oligarch regards the jurors as men of the people ([Xen.] *Ath. Pol.* i. 16-18), and Aristotle comments that the introduction of pay meant that ordinary people put in to be jurors rather than the respectable classes (*Ath. Pol.* 27. 4).

¹⁴⁸ See above, pp. 19, 36–7.

¹⁴⁹ Thuc. VI. 8. 2, 26. 1. For other magistrates see Tod, I. 44 (the founder of a colony); for envoys, Andoc. III. 33, αὐτοκράτορας γὰρ πεμφθῆναι εἰς Λακεδαίμονα διὰ ταῦθ᾽ ἵνα μὴ πάλιν ἐπαναφέρωμεν; for the council, Tod, I. 51, SEG X. 64a, 84, cf. Dem. XIX. 154, Andoc. I. 15.

¹⁵⁰ Thuc. IV. 66, 76.

¹⁵¹ Thuc. IV. 118. 14. Cf. SEG X. 84.

¹⁵² SEG X. 86.

¹⁵³ *Syll.*³ 132.

¹⁵⁴ Tod, I. 61, line 55, cf. Arist. *Ath. Pol.* 30. 5.

¹⁵⁵ *IG* II-III.² 108, Tod, II. 143.

¹⁵⁶ Thuc. VI. 25. 1.

¹⁵⁷ Thuc. VI. 43. 2, 44. 3-45, 52. 2.

¹⁵⁸ Thuc. I. 116. 1, II. 13. 1.

¹⁵⁹ The evidence is fully set out in C. Hignett, *A History of the Athenian Constitution*, Appendix XI, pp. 347-56. I am indebted to Mr. D. M. Lewis for the probable addition of 126 to the list.

¹⁶⁰ Dem. XVIII. 149, προβληθεὶς πυλάγορος οὗτος καὶ τριῶν ἢ τεττάρων χειροτονησάντων αὐτὸν ἀνερρήθη, 285, ὁ δῆμος. . . οὐ σὲ ἐχειροτόνησε προβληθέντα, Aesch. II. 18, ψήφισμα ἔγραψεν ὁ Φιλοκράτης ἑλέσθαι πρέσβεις πρὸς Φίλιππον ἄνδρας δέκα... χειροτονουμένων δὲ τῶν δέκα πρεσβευτῶν ἐγὼ μὲν προεβλήθην ὑπὸ Ναυσικλέους, Δημοσθένης δ᾽ ὑπ᾽ αὐτοῦ Φιλοκράτους, cf. Dem. XXI. 15,200. See Arist. *Ath. Pol.* 44. 4 for the probouleuma for elections.

¹⁶¹ Arist. *Ath. Pol.* 22. 2, 61. 1. Nomination by tribes would be analogous with the procedure for appointing choregi (Arist. *Ath. Pol.* 56. 3, Dem. XXI. 13). Demes were sometimes represented in the council by members of other demes (see above, note 69) by a similar arrangement.

¹⁶² Thuc. II. 22. 1.

¹⁶³ Thuc. II. 65. 8.

¹⁶⁴ Thuc. II. 65. 3-4.

¹⁶⁵ Thuc. II. 59. 2.

¹⁶⁶ Dem. IV. 26.

¹⁶⁷ Demades, 9.

¹⁶⁸ Hypereides, I. 24-25. Cf. Dem. LVIII. 35.

¹⁶⁹ Arist. *Ath. Pol.* 43. 1.

[170] Aesch. III. 25.

[171] His precise title is unknown. Hypereides says that he was ταχθεὶς ἐπὶ τῇ διοικήσει τῶν χρημάτων (fr. 118) and that the people elected him ἐπὶ τὴν διοίκησιν τῶν αὐτοῦ ἅπασαν ταμίαν (I.28). Demosthenes says that he αὐτὸν ἐν τῷ περὶ τὴν διοίκησιν μέρει τάξας τῆς πολιτείας (Ep. iii. 2). In the garbled decree in [Plut.] Vit. X. Or. (Mor. 852 A) he is styled τῆς κοινῆς προσόδου ταμίας.

[172] Arist. Ath. Pol. 47. 2, cf. 49. 3.

[173] Aesch. III. 25.

[174] Diodorus (XVI. 88) speaks of him as τὰς προσόδους τῆς πόλεως διοικήσας for twelve years, and the decree cited in note 171 says that he was τῆς κοινῆς προσόδου ταμίας τῇ πόλει ἐπὶ τρεῖς πενταετηρίδας, but in the Life of Lycurgus ([Plut.] Mor. 841 B) it is explained that he actually held office for one quadrennium only.

[175] Dem. III. 30.

[176] Ib. XXII. 37.

[177] Ib. LVIII. 39-40.

[178] See above, pp. 23 ff.

[179] Dem. II. 29, XIII. 20. Cf. Aesch. III. 7.

[180] See R. Sealey in JHS 1955, 74-81.

[181] Arist. Ath. Pol. 28.

[182] Dem. XXI. 208 ff.

[183] Hell. Oxy. i 2-3.

[184] Diod. XVIII. 10.

[185] Aristoph. Eccl. 197-8.

[186] Deinarchus, in Dem. 72.

[187] Plato, Protagoras, 319b-323a cited on pp. 46 7 above.

[188] Xen. Mem. III. vi.

APPENDIX

The Citizen Population of Athens during the Peloponnesian War

IN THE first quarter of the fifth century the adult male citizen population of Athens would seem from the meagre and imprecise data available to have numbered about 30,000, of whom about 10,000 were hoplites; under which term I include, unless otherwise stated or implied, the cavalry (see above, p.8). During the period between the Persian and Peloponnesian wars we have one figure only, and that not a very useful one. For the battle of Tanagra (458 or 457) the Athenians raised a hoplite army of 14,000: they themselves served in full force (πανδημεί) and they had with them 1,000 Argives and other allies (Thuc. I. 107. 5). There were at this date some Athenian hoplites, but probably not many, engaged elsewhere, at Aegina and in Egypt. These figures imply that the Athenian hoplite force had risen somewhat, perhaps by 25 per cent., above 10,000.

For the year 431 Thucydides (II. 13. 6-8) gives us full hoplite statistics. Pericles reminded the people 'that there were 13,000 hoplites apart from the 16,000 in the forts and on the walls. For as many as that at first kept guard whenever the enemy invaded, from the oldest and the youngest, and all the metic hoplites. For there were 35 stades of the Phaleric wall . . .' Thucydides proceeds to give a detailed description, showing that there were in all 148 stades (over 16 miles) of wall to patrol. He then mentions the 1,200 cavalry, including the mounted archers; 1,000 of them will have been the real cavalry, drawn from the highest census classes and to be added to the hoplite total.

These are startling figures, and many attempts have been made to get round them. Some have misinterpreted Thucydides' words, by making the 16,000 include the thetes (Delbrück,

Geschichte der Kriegskunst, I. 15-24). Others have amended the text, either reducing the 16,000 to 6,000 (Beloch, *Klio* V (1905), 356-74, Busolt, *Griechische Geschichte*, III. ii. 878-88, *Griechische Staatskunde*, II. 764-6), or adding colonists to the metics to fill out the 16,000 (Beloch, *Die Bevölkerung der griechisch-römischen Welt*, 60-66). But Thucydides' language is explicit, and the figures cannot be rejected as textual errors. That of 13,000 for the field army is confirmed by Thucydides himself in a later passage (II. 31. 2), where he records that 10,000 Athenian hoplites took part in the invasion of the Megarid, while 3,000 were at Potidaea. Diodorus (that is, Ephorus), moreover, gives the same gross total, divided into '12,000 hoplites and more than 17,000 garrison troops and metics' (Diod. XII. 40. 4).

The figures raise two main difficulties: first the apparent disproportion between the field army, comprising the active service age groups, and the defence army, consisting of the oldest and youngest and metics; and secondly the very large gross total, as compared with earlier and later figures. There is also a third minor difficulty, the proportion between the number of deaths from the plague among the cavalry and the hoplites.

Only one explanation of the first difficulty has been offered, that of Professor Gomme in *CQ.* XXI (1927), 142-151, repeated in his *Population of Athens*, pp. 4-5. Gomme suggests that there were many men in the active service age groups (which he takes to have been 20-49) who were unfit for the field army but capable of garrison duty, and that these men were classed with the youngest (18-19) and oldest (50-59).

There are serious objections to this theory. It is in the first place not what Thucydides says. Secondly it is a pure speculation, unsupported by any evidence. The Athenians recognised the unfit (ἀδύνατοι), who were presumably totally exempt, but these were men obviously incapable of fighting at all, lame like Lysias' client in Oration XXIV or blind like Timarchus' uncle (Aesch. I. 102-4). A man might also presumably be excused on a particular occasion if he were ill at the time, like the two Spartans

who were sent back to base from Thermopylae because of an
attack of ophthalmia (Herod. VII. 229). We know of no case
at Athens, but we may conjecture that in such circumstances a
man would, like Aeschines when he wished to evade an embassy,
send in an affidavit (ἐξωμοσία) backed by a doctor's certificate
(Dem. XIX. 124). The Athenians also recognised that service in
the cavalry demanded an exceptional standard of physical fitness,
and members of the corps or those designated to serve could, by
an affidavit that they were physically unfit for cavalry service,
get themselves removed from the list (Arist. *Ath. Pol.* 49.2,
cf. Xen. *Hipparch.* ix. 5), presumably becoming hoplites unless
totally incapacitated. But there was only one hoplite register
(κατάλογος). In this sense the word is always used in the
singular, as in Thuc. VI. 43, VII. 16. 1, 20. 2, VIII. 24. 2, cf. Xen.
Mem. III. iv. 1 and Dem. XIII. 4, ὑπὲρ τὸν κατάλογον, explained
by Pollux, II. 11, as over 60; the plural κατάλογοι in Thuc. VI.
26. 2, 31. 3, bears a different meaning—selective call-up within
this single register. The men were listed in year groups, 42 in
all from 18 to 59 (Arist. *Ath. Pol.* 53. 4), and the call-up, unless
it was selective (ἐν τοῖς μέρεσιν), was by year groups (ἐν τοῖς
ἐπωνύμοις, Arist. *Ath. Pol.* 53. 7 and Aesch. II. 168, cf. Lysias,
XIV. 6). Neither at Athens nor anywhere else in the ancient
world is it recorded that liability for active or defence service
was regulated by any other criterion but age.

Let us then set aside this theory and examine the facts afresh.
Thucydides' language implies that because of the exceptionally
heavy demands of defence, the number of men allocated to it was
increased during these years. This again implies that the rules
governing the employment of the oldest and youngest and of
the metics were not rigid but might vary according to circumstances.

As to the youngest there can be no dispute. What is meant is
the 18- and 19-year-old classes, the ephebes. About the oldest
there is room for doubt. It is usually stated on the strength of a
statement by Lycurgus (*c. Leocratem*, 39-40) that they were the

50-59 classes. But this passage merely proves that for the battle of Chaeroneia, an extreme emergency, all men up to 50 were called up, so that the defence of the city was left to the over 50 classes. For the expedition to Thermopylae in 347, on the other hand, it was decided to mobilise men up to 40 only (Aesch. II. 133; some MSS. give 30), and so too for the Lamian war (Diod. XVIII. 10). An anecdote in Plutarch's *Phocion* (ch. 24) implies that theoretically all men up to 60 might be called up for active service. Our evidence in fact suggests that there was no fixed age limit for active service, and that the call-up was adjusted according to the needs of the situation. In 431 the 20-39s may have been allocated (as in the Lamian war) to the field army, and the 40-59s (with the 18-19s) to home defence.

It is also generally stated that the metics were normally called up for home defence only. This doctrine, however, rests on the present passage only. Metics were certainly employed regularly on foreign service in the fourth century, as appears from Xenophon's proposal for their exemption from hoplite service (*de Vect.* ii. 2-5). In the fifth century they were called up for Delium (Thuc. IV. 90. 1), and 3,000 were employed in this very year for the invasion of the Megarid (Thuc. II. 31. 2). It would seem that in principle and in practice metics were liable to service abroad, and that it was exceptional to reserve them for home defence, as in 431.

On the number of metic hoplites we have no evidence. There is, as Gomme has pointed out, no justification for assuming that the 3,000 who served in the Megarid represent the whole number of metic hoplites, or even all those in the active service age groups. It is hardly a coincidence that 3,000 metics were called up at a time when 3,000 Athenians were detained at Potidaea (Thuc. II. 31. 2): only so many metics were levied for the Megarid campaign as would bring the invading army up to full strength. On general grounds of probability it may be conjectured that the number of metic hoplites was far in excess of 3,000. A century later, under Demetrius of Phaleron, the metics numbered 10,000, nearly half the contemporary citizen total of 21,000 (Athenaeus, VI. 272c). In 431, when Athens was far more prosperous, the number is likely to have been considerably greater, with a high proportion of hoplites.

It has been argued above (see pp. 82-3) that there is reason to believe that the age distribution of the Athenian population was similar to that worked out by Mr. A. R. Burn for various areas of the Roman Empire. On this assumption, if 14,000 (the hoplite field army and the cavalry) represent the 20-39 age groups, the 40-59s will have amounted to slightly under half that figure, rather less than 7,000. The two very large ephebic classes would have totalled rather over 2,000. There will then have been 9,000 citizens in the garrison army, and we are left with 7,000 metic hoplites, which seems not unreasonable. The total number of citizens of military age and hoplite census will then have been 23,000, or not counting the ephebes, 21,000.

It will be convenient to deal at this stage with the third difficulty. Under the year 427 Thucydides (III. 87. 3) states that 'no fewer than 4,400 hoplites from the regiments (ἐκ τῶν τάξεων) and 300 cavalry died (of the plague from 430 to 427) and an incalculable number of the remainder of the population'. It has been argued that if the hoplites were as numerous as Thucydides' figures imply (22,000 including the ephebes by my calculations), the proportion of deaths among them (20 per cent.) is too low as compared with the proportion among the cavalry (30 per cent.), especially as the latter, being all young men, might have been expected to suffer less. Gomme endeavours to solve this difficulty by postulating that the phrase 'hoplites from the regiments' means the field army of 13,000 (giving a proportion of 34 per cent. deaths), but this is illegitimate. It is certain that all hoplites (with the possible exception of the ephebes) were entered in the tribal regiments (τάξεις), and the contrast between the exact numbers given for the hoplites and cavalry and the 'incalculable number' for the rest of the population shows that Thucydides is dealing on the one hand with the classes of the citizens of whom a register was kept (that is the cavalry and all the hoplites), and the thetes, who were at this period not entered on any unified list, and among whom therefore the number of deaths was not recorded. The phrase 'from the regiments' is presumably added either to exclude the ephebes, or more probably thetes equipped as hoplites for service in the fleet as marines. The proportion of 20 per cent. deaths among the hoplites must then stand.

But the whole argument is very flimsy. We do not know in the first place whether mortality was more severe among the old or the young. And in the second place the 1,000 cavalry are a very small sample on which to base an average. The corps may well for accidental reasons have suffered abnormally. Hagnon's hoplite army at Potidaea, Thucydides tells us (II. 58. 3), lost 1,050 men out of 4,000 (26 per cent.) in forty days. The corps of cavalry, which was constantly mobilised during this period, may well have suffered such an acute epidemic.

To turn to the second difficulty, the number of hoplites will, if my interpretation of Thucydides' figures is correct, have approximately doubled in the fifty years since the Persian wars. This is a striking but not impossible increase. Since hoplite status depended on the assessed value of a man's property (see p. 142, note 50), it implies primarily an evenly distributed increase in wealth as assessed in money. This is *a priori* probable in mid-fifth-century Athens. The thetes were earning good money in State service (primarily as rowers) and in industry, which was thriving, and in particular in the great programme of public works. Some will have been able to invest in enough slaves or house property to qualify as hoplites.

Besides the real increase in wealth there was probably a fictitious increase due to an inflationary trend. From 483 the Laurium mines were producing large quantities of silver, and from the foundation of the Delian League, and especially from 449, when the reserve fund began to be spent on public works, considerable sums of tribute money were pumped into the Athenian economy. Prices must have risen, and our tenuous evidence suggests that they did. In a Solonian law a drachma was equated with a medimnus (Plut. *Solon*, 23. 3), and there seems no reason why prices should have risen in the next century. By the beginning of the fourth century, if we may take seriously an allusion in Aristophanes (*Eccl.* 547-8), wheat stood at 3 drachmae the medimnus. Assessments no doubt lagged behind prices, but the revaluation of property must have brought some thetes into the hoplite class, in the way that Aristotle (*Pol.* 1306b) remarks was liable to happen in times of prosperity.

These two factors, the real increase of personal and of house property and the apparent increase in the value of all property, including land, must have increased the number of hoplites, but it is difficult to believe that they alone can have doubled it. Many thetes must also have acquired land. Redistribution of land in Attica would not, of course, affect the issue unless large estates were broken up, for which there is not a scrap of evidence. Land must have been acquired abroad. There are two ways in which this could have happened, by private acquisition and by state action.

The first possibility has been strangely ignored. In the charter of the Second Athenian League (Tod. II. 123) there is a clause which has been generally interpreted as a guarantee against Athenian cleruchies. But if so it is very strangely phrased: 'And that from the archonship of Nausinicus it be not lawful for any Athenian to acquire a house or land in the territories of the allies either privately or publicly either by purchase or mortgage or in any other way'. Cleruchies would no doubt be covered by the word 'publicly', but what the potential allies of Athens evidently feared more was private purchase or mortgage. This implies that many Athenians had in the days of the Delian League exploited their predominant position to claim the right of land ownership (γῆς ἔγκτησις) in the territories of the allies.

It may however be doubted whether the private acquisition of land abroad by Athenian citizens greatly affected the total of hoplites; for the majority of the purchasers or mortgagees would probably have been well-to-do men already in the hoplite class. This brings us to the question of cleruchies and colonies. This problem is fully discussed in *The Athenian Tribute Lists*, III, 282-297, a passage to which I owe much.

In both the inscriptions (e.g. *IG* I². 140) and the literary authorities a distinction is drawn (though in the latter, especially the late secondary sources, it is often blurred) between colonies (ἀποικίαι) and colonists (ἄποικοι, sometimes called, when the reference is to their initial despatch, ἔποικοι) on the one hand, and cleruchies (κληρουχίαι) and cleruchs (κληροῦχοι) on the other. There is scarcely any fifth-century evidence on the significance of the distinction, but on the analogy of general Greek practice it may be assumed that a colony was, technically at any rate, an independent State, and that the colonists ceased to be Athenian citizens and became citizens of the colony. Cleruchs, on the other hand, in the fourth century certainly remained Athenian citizens, and may be presumed to have done so in the fifth.

The effect of planting a colony was therefore to diminish the number of Athenian citizens, but not necessarily the number of Athenian hoplites. For the majority of the settlers were probably thetes. The amendment to the decree relating to the foundation of the colony of Brea, 'that the colonists for Brea be from the thetes and zeugites' (Tod. I. 44), is probably to be interpreted, as Mr. de Ste Croix has suggested to me, as making the zeugites eligible in addition to the thetes (who had been specified in the lost opening paragraphs of the decree), rather than as restricting participation in the colony to the two lowest classes; for it is hardly likely that many rich Athenians would have wished to leave Athens (and abandon their citizenship) to settle in the wilds of Thrace. A cleruchy, on the other hand, would leave the number of citizens unchanged but would raise some from thetic to zeugite rank. For once again the majority of cleruchs were probably by origin thetes, and in the one case in which we know the value of the allotments, at Lesbos (Thuc. III. 50. 2), they brought in a rent of 200 drachmae a year, which was probably equivalent to the minimum zeugite qualification (see above, p. 142, note 50).

Not only were thetes thus converted into zeugites, but zeugites were prevented from sinking to thetic status. When a poor zeugite left more than one son, the sons would, according to general practice, divide the property equally, and thus both or all become thetes. But if the father or one or more of the sons acquired allotments, there would be property enough for two or more sons all to maintain their zeugite qualification. Colonies would have had a similar effect: if the second son of a poor zeugite joined a colony, his brother would succeed to the whole of his father's farm. In a period when, as I shall argue later, the population was expanding rapidly, the number of hoplites might, but for this, have sunk by the splitting up of small farms.

It is not in all cases possible to distinguish which settlements were colonies and which cleruchies. Besides Thurii (443) and Amphipolis (437), in which Athenian settlers were in a minority, the following very probably were colonies:

Histiaea (446). Thuc. VII. 57. 2. In another passage (VIII. 95. 7) he alludes to the population as Athenians, but he is presumably thinking not of their legal status but of their origins. Diodorus (XII. 22) also calls it a colony, and adds τήν τε πόλιν καὶ τὴν χώραν κατεκληρούχησαν, but this is not inconsistent, for in a colony the houses and land had to be divided into lots for the settlers: Diodorus uses the same phrase in describing the foundation of Amphipolis (XI. 70. 5). He gives the number of settlers as 1,000. Theopompus (fr. 387 in *F. Gr. Hist.*) gives 2,000 settlers.

Brea (*c.* 445). Tod. I. 44. Plutarch (*Pericles*, 11) gives the number of settlers as 1,000.

Aegina (431). Thuc. II. 27. 1, VIII. 69. 3 and perhaps VII. 57. 2. Numbers not recorded.

Potidaea (430). Thuc. II. 70. 4, Tod, I. 60. Diodorus (XII. 46) uses the same phrase as with Histiaea and gives the number as 1,000.

Melos (416). Thuc. V. 116. 4. 500 settlers.

The 600 Athenian settlers at Sinope (Plut. *Pericles*, 20) presumably became Sinopians, and the settlers at Amisus (Theopompus, fr. 389, cf. Plut. *Lucullus*, 19, Appian, *Mithr.* 83) also presumably became citizens of the town, refounded as Peiraeus. Astacus (Memnon, fr. 12, Diod, XII. 34, Strabo, 563) was also refounded with additional settlers. An inscription (*Syll.*³ 65) records τῆς ἀποι[κίας] τῆς ἐς 'Eϱ. . . . This has been restored as Eretria, Eresos or Erythrae. The last is perhaps the most probable: it may be doubted whether the 'colony' was more than a reinforcement of the population of Erythrae, which may have been officially refounded. Another inscription (*SEG.* X. 17) mentions οἰκισταί in connection with Colophon. This again probably only means that Colophon was officially refounded with additional settlers. It might also mean that cleruchs were sent to Colophon: in the fourth century οἰκισταί were sent to the Chersonese (*IG.* II-III². 1613, 297-8), which was then certainly a cleruchy (Dem. VIII. 6, cf. XXIII. 103 and Aesch. II. 72).

The following were fairly certainly cleruchies:

Naxos, Andros and a place in Euboea (Carystus?) (449). Plutarch (*Pericles*, 11) states that Pericles planted 500 cleruchs in Naxos and 250 in Andros: as his list includes undoubted colonies the passage is dubious evidence for the legal status of the settlers. Diodorus (XI. 88) states that Tolmides went to Euboea and distributed the land of the Naxians to 1,000 citizens. A lacuna is suspected in the text; the 1,000 settlers were probably distributed between Naxos (500), Andros (250) and a place (or places) in Euboea (250). As in 449 the tribute of Carystus was reduced from 7½ to 5 talents, and that of Andros from 12 to 6 (the earliest figure for Naxos is 6⅔ in 447, which is low for an island of this size, and implies a similar reduction), it is inferred that land was taken from these cities (and perhaps others in Euboea for which figures are lacking) for the Athenian settlers. Diodorus' words imply cleruchies. The settlers certainly did not become Naxians, Andrians and Carystians(?), for in that case there would have been no reason to reduce the tribute of these cities; and 250 is surely too small for an independent colony.

Chalcis (446). Aelian, *Var. Hist.* VI. 1, Ἀθηναῖοι κρατήσαντες Χαλκιδέων κατεκληρούχησαν αὐτῶν τὴν γῆν εἰς δισχιλίους κλήρους, τὴν Ἱπποβοτῶν καλουμένην χώραν (cf. Plut. *Pericles*, 23, for the expulsion of the Hippobotae in 446). Probably 1,800 cleruchs, allowing for the share (presumably a tenth as at Lesbos: Thuc. III. 50. 2) dedicated according to Aelian to Athena.

Lesbos (427). Thuc. III. 50. 2, Tod. I, 63. 3,000 lots and 2,7000 cleruchs (300 lots to the gods).

The Chersonese is a doubtful case. Plutarch in one passage (*Pericles*, 11) speaks of 1,000 cleruchs, and in another (op. cit. 19) of 1,000 colonists. Diodorus (XI. 88) says χιλίοις τῶν πολιτῶν κατεκληρούχησε τὴν χώραν; this in view of the parallel passages about Naxos, Histiaea and Potidaea is of doubtful value. The tribute of the Chersonesite cities was reduced from 18 talents in 451 to 13 talents 4,840 drachmae in 449 (perhaps owing to the Thracian devastations), and later (the change is first traceable in 442) to only 1 talent. This does not affect the question of cleruchy or colony, as land must have been surrendered for either.

Finally there are Lemnos, Imbros and Scyros. These three islands were regarded in the fourth century as virtually appanages of Attica. Made independent on the fall of Athens (Andoc. III. 12), they were within a decade in Athenian hands again (Xen. *Hell.* IV. viii. 15) and were recognised as Athenian possessions by the King's Peace (ib. V. i. 31). They were at this period cleruchies, the communities being styled ὁ δῆμος ὁ Ἀθηναίων ὁ ἐν Ἴμβρῳ οἰκῶν and the like for Scyros and the two Lemnian cities, Hephaestia and Myrina (*IG.* XII. 8. 3 ff., 26, 46, 668). This proves nothing about their status in the fifth century, for in the fourth all Athenian outsettlements (except for a colony sent to the Adriatic, Tod. II. 200) were cleruchies (e.g. Aesch. I. 53,

*Syll.*³. 276 for Samos: Dem. VIII. 6, XXIII. 103, Aesch. II. 72 for the Chersonese; Tod. II. 146 for Potidaea). The fourth-century evidence does however suggest that the whole population of the islands was Athenian by descent.

Scyros. Cimon expelled the natives and settled it with Athenians c. 473 (Thuc. I. 98. 2, Plut. *Cimon*, 8, Diod. XI. 60). Both Thucydides and Plutarch use the neutral word οἰκίζειν. Diodorus says κτιστὴν Ἀθηναῖον καταστήσας κατεκληρούχησε τὴν γῆν. The use of the verb κατακληρουχεῖν is, as noted above, indecisive. A founder (κτιστής) might imply a colony, but, as we have seen, οἰκισταί were in the fourth century sent to establish a cleruchy.

Lemnos and Imbros. The Pelasgian inhabitants of Hephaestia and Myrina were expelled by Miltiades before the Persian wars, and Athenian settlers substituted (Herod. VI. 136, 140), and the same was probably done at Imbros (this is implied by Herod. V. 26, cf. VI. 41 and 104). An inscription from Hephaestia which must be dated before the Persian wars (*BCH*, XXXVI (1912), 330-38) gives a list of names arranged in the Athenian tribes. This might equally well mean that the city was inhabited by cleruchs, still in their Athenian tribes, or that Hephaestia, as a colony of Athens, had tribes of the same names as the Athenian. The two Lemnian cities and Imbros paid tribute in the Delian League. The cities which paid tribute can hardly be, as had been suggested, the Pelasgians, for all the evidence indicates that they were completely expelled or exterminated. They must then be Athenian colonies, for cleruchs, being Athenian citizens, could not pay separately. Other Athenian colonies, founded after the inception of the Delian League, did not, it is true, pay tribute either. But these old colonies may have been assessed by Aristeides, correctly from the constitutional point of view, and the rule changed later.

In 449 the Lemnians, who in 451 had paid 9 talents, were (probably) assessed at 3 for Hephaestia and 1 for Myrina (from 443 certainly 3 and 1½). This has been taken to mean that they surrendered land to Athenian cleruchs; but it would be very odd for the Athenians to have planted cleruchs in the islands instead of reinforcing the colonists, and other explanations are possible for the reduction in tribute. Members of this supposed second batch of settlers have also been seen in two mid-fifth-century lists from Athens (*IG* I², 947-8), where 'Lemnians' or 'Lemnians from Myrina' are recorded under Athenian tribes. But it is also possible that lists of Lemnian colonists in their own (identical) tribes, probably those who died fighting for Athens, may have been set up in the mother city.

This list suggests that colonies were sent either (*a*) as at Amisus and Sinope (and Thurii), to reinforce existing cities (and to strengthen the pro-Athenian party in them), or (*b*) as at Histiaea, Potidaea, Aegina and Melos, to occupy the sites of enemy cities destroyed, or (*c*) as at Brea (and Amphipolis) to occupy strategic points on barbarian soil. On these principles Scyros was probably a colony of type (*b*). Cleruchies were planted in the territory of an existing city. The land was obtained at Chalcis by the confiscation of the estates of the anti-Athenian oligarchy. It may be conjectured that the land at Naxos and Carystus (?) had been confiscated after the reduction of those two cities, and was now utilised for allotment.

In the Chersonese Plutarch (*Pericles*, 19) suggests that the Athenian settlers occupied waste lands in the cities, which had suffered greatly from Thracian raids. Since the settlers were not enrolled in the cities (as the reductions of tribute show), they were probably cleruchs.

To return to the population of Athens, on this reckoning several thousands of Athenians were despatched as colonists during the Pentecontaetia, and ceased thereby to be citizens: the number cannot be calculated, as no figures have survived except the 600 at Sinope and 1,000 at Brea and 1,000 or 2,000 at Histiaea. Several thousand Athenian citizens were also given allotments in cleruchies and thereby raised to or maintained in zeugite status. If the Chersonese be reckoned a cleruchy the minimum figure is

3,800. Are these 4,000 (or, if the Chersonese was a colony, 3,000) odd hoplites to be included in Thucydides' figures or not?

It is the generally accepted doctrine that cleruchies were regarded as garrisons, and that cleruchs were therefore not liable to military service outside the territory in which they were planted. On this assumption Gomme very properly excludes cleruchs altogether from the hoplite strength given by Thucydides as available for field service and for the defence of the walls of Athens and the forts of Attica.

The accepted doctrine is, however, based on very tenuous evidence. It rests in fact on two passages, one in Plutarch's Life of Pericles (11. 7) and the other in Isocrates' Panegyricus (IV. 107). Plutarch states that the objects of the policy of colonies and cleruchies (which he does not distinguish) was two-fold, on the one hand to drain Athens of its unemployed and relieve the poverty of the people, and on the other to provide a deterrent and a garrison to prevent allied revolts. Plutarch's opinions on Athenian policy are not of great value in any case, and his failure to distinguish cleruchies and colonies, the latter of which might be regarded as strategical strongpoints, makes his evidence on the particular point at issue of even less value. Isocrates is concerned to prove that the Athenians did not act from self-interested motives in planting cleruchies, 'which we sent out to those cities which were depopulated to protect the places, not from greed'. Isocrates' argument is highly tendentious. He had to find a disinterested motive for cleruchies, and he finds it in rather vague strategical needs—for it is not clear against whom the places required to be protected in his view; as the allies were according to him perfectly contented, presumably against external enemies.

This is apparently the sole evidence that the cleruchies were intended to serve as garrisons, and that the cleruchs were therefore reserved for the defence of these settlements and not liable to general military service. If that was the intention of the cleruchies they do not seem to have fulfilled it very efficiently. After the fall of Mitylene in 427, 2,700 cleruchs were 'sent out' to Lesbos, but three years later, in 424, Mitylenaean exiles were able to seize Rhoeteum and Antandrus and raid Lesbos (Thuc. IV. 52); Thucydides records no opposition by the cleruch garrison. In 411 the Chians brought about the revolt of Methymna and Mitylene, and again no opposition is recorded (VIII. 22). In Euboea 2,000 cleruchs had been planted in Chalcidian territory in 446, but in 411 the Peloponnesians after the battle of Eretria brought about the revolt of the whole island except Oreus, and the explanation of the exception is that the Athenians themselves (that is, the Athenian colonists of Histiaea) held it (VIII. 95. 7). The implication is clear that there were no Athenians holding Chalcis.

These two instances prove either that the cleruchs of military age were away on active service or garrison duty elsewhere, or that they did not reside on their lots at all. The latter is perhaps the likelier alternative, seeing that no cleruch families are mentioned as suffering when Euboea and Lesbos revolted in 411. In the old days before the Persian wars the 4,000 cleruchs who were allotted the lands of the Chalcidian hippobotae certainly did settle in Euboea, as Herodotus' narrative of the events of 490 proves (Herod. V. 77, VI. 100-01). Thucydides says that the Athenians 'sent out' (ἀπέπεμψαν) cleruchs to Lesbos, but one may wonder whether 'to send out' was not by now a term of art.

A very mutilated inscription (Tod, I. 63) has been taken to prove that Athenian cleruchs actually went to Lesbos, but the fragments actually demonstrate nothing more than that the Mitylenaeans had some dealings with cleruchs, which would have been the case whether the latter were resident or not. Gomme (*A Historical Commentary on Thucydides*, II, 328-32) has, on the basis of a (necessarily) very hypothetical reconstruction of this inscription, proposed a theory that the cleruchs, having gone out in 427, were withdrawn, and the land restored to the Mitylenaeans, before 424. But Thucydides would hardly have omitted so striking and sudden a reversal of policy. It seems more likely that the cleruchs stayed at home and that the Lesbians (presumably the old tenants of the oligarchic landlords) worked the land and paid them their fixed rent. Why should they not draw their rents at Athens, instead of living in an alien land (and where were the houses for them to live in?). The same conditions probably applied in Chalcis. In Naxos we hear of an Athenian family residing (Plato, *Euthyphro*, 4c), but it is not stated that they were cleruchs. They were evidently well off, employing slaves and hired labour on their farm, and may have been private owners of a large estate which they had bought. Eutherus had also resided abroad until the fall of Athens, and had then been reduced to poverty, 'since we were deprived of our lands overseas, and my father left me nothing in Attica' (Xen. *Mem.* II. viii. 1). But he too is not stated to have been a cleruch, and seems to have come from a well-off family, owning land both in Attica and several places abroad. There is in fact no clear evidence of an Athenian cleruch residing on his lot overseas during the Pentecontaetia and the Peloponnesian war. I would suggest that they were not obliged or expected to do so, and that the allotments were regarded as endowments which qualified them for hoplite service: they might prefer to cultivate them themselves, but they seem normally to have been absentee landlords.

A priori it would seem natural that the Athenians, when they sent out some citizens as colonists and some as cleruchs, deleting the former from the citizen roll and maintaining the latter on it, intended that the latter should continue to perform their civic duties, one of the most important of which was military service. It would have been a fantastic waste of man power to sterilise 2,700 able-bodied citizens as a permanent garrison of Lesbos, and almost as fantastic to allocate 1,800 to hold Chalcis, to which the Athenian army could cross any day, while Naxos and Andros do not appear to have needed garrisons at all.

There is unfortunately no clear and explicit evidence whether in fact cleruchs served or no. Thucydides mentions that in Sicily besides the Athenians themselves there were 'still using the same language and customs as they, Lemnians and Imbrians, and Aeginetans (who then occupied Aegina), and moreover Histiaeans who inhabited Histiaea in Euboea, colonists' (VII. 57. 2). It is a matter of taste how this sentence is punctuated, but all four communities were colonies, the Lemnians and Imbrians being clearly the old colonists, who had been so long separated from Athens that it was noteworthy that they still kept up Athenian speech and manners, and not the putative cleruchs of later date. Thucydides elsewhere (V. 74. 3, VIII. 69. 3) twice mentions Aeginetan colonists serving, and on several occasions Lemnians and Imbrians. These, 'with some few of the other allies', assisted Athens in the revolt of Mitylene (III. 5. 1). Cleon said that he would take with him to Pylos no one from Athens, but 'the Lemnians and Imbrians who were there' (IV. 28. 4), and 'the best troops of the Lemnians and Imbrians' served under him in the Amphipolis campaign (V. 8. 2). Thucydides does not record the presence of cleruchs in the Athenian forces, either because they did not serve, or more probably because they served in the normal course as citizens. I would therefore argue that the 3,000 or 4,000 cleruchs were called up for service in the appropriate age groups, and either fought in the field army or helped to man the walls and forts. If this thesis is accepted the very high hoplite total given by Thucydides for 431 becomes more plausible.

Besides the increase in wealth during the Pentecontaetia, which so greatly increased the hoplite class, there must also have been a very considerable increase in population. We have no figures for the thetic class, but on general grounds (see above p. 9) it is to be inferred that despite the promotion of some thousands to the hoplite class and the drafting of several thousands to colonies, it maintained its numbers at about 20,000 if it did not increase them. This is not impossible or indeed surprising. Modern populations of the same pattern as the Athenian—those of Egypt and India, for instance—respond very rapidly to economic prosperity. The birth rate is high, and the population is only kept down by high mortality. If there is more food available, more survive and the population leaps up rapidly.

It is somewhat surprising, in view of these figures, that at Delium in 424 the Athenians were able to muster a hoplite force of only 7,000, although they held a levy in full force (πανδημεί), including not only metics but non-resident foreigners (Thuc. IV. 90. 1, 93. 3, 94. 1). We do not know what precisely 'in full force' means in this context, but the phrase probably refers to all classes rather than all age groups (IV. 94. 1, πανστρατιᾶς ξένων τῶν παρόντων καὶ ἀστῶν γενομένης; similarly the invasion of the Megarid in 431 is stated in II. 31 to have been πανστρατιᾷ although less than half the hoplites, with many light-armed, took part): for a large number of thetes were mustered to build the fortified post at Delium (IV. 90. 4, 94. 1, 101. 2). But hoplites were certainly mustered up to 45 at least, since Socrates served (Plut. *Alcibiades*, 7). The plague had, of course, intervened, carrying off 4,400 hoplites and 300 cavalry, and no doubt maiming many more—Thucydides records that many who recovered lost their hands or feet or their eyesight (II. 49. 8). The low number mustered at Delium is however probably to be explained chiefly by the fact that secrecy was of the essence of the operation, and that no previous notice of the call-up can have been given, so that many hoplites in outlying demes may not have received their summons in time.

The next figure which we possess is the 9,000 who were enrolled in 411 in the register of the "Five Thousand" (Ps.-Lysias, XX, 13). This again is a surprisingly low figure. The figure would presumably include those over 60, who can hardly have been deprived of political rights. It has been argued (by Ferguson in *C.A.H.* V. 338, supported by Gomme, *Population of Athens*, 7) that it included only those over thirty. There is however no justification for this view. Neither in Thucydides nor in Aristotle (*Ath. Pol.* 29. 5 and 30) is any age qualification suggested for the "Five Thousand"; it is only the councillors drawn from this body who are to be over 30. One must assume that all over 20 were eligible. About 800 out of 9,000 would be over 60, leaving 8,200 from 20 to 59. There had, it is true, been heavy casualties since 424; 1,000 hoplites fell in that year at Delium (Thuc. IV. 101. 2), 600 more at Amphipolis (V. 11. 2), and 2,700 sailed for Sicily (VI. 43, VII. 20. 2), very few of whom ever returned. The effects of the plague, which recurred seriously in the winter of 427-6 (III. 87. 1-2), will moreover still have been felt, if children were affected as much as adults. Nevertheless the drop is startling from 21,000 in 431, if 8,200 represents all Athenians of zeugite status between 20 and 59. It is, however, noteworthy that the simple criterion of zeugite census is never mentioned in the story of the revolution. In the early stages it was proposed that the "Five Thousand" were to comprise 'those best able to serve with their money and their persons' (*Ath. Pol.* 29. 5, Thuc. VIII, 65. 3), and after the fall of the Four Hundred this phrase is clarified as 'those who provide arms' (Thuc. VIII. 97. 1). It would appear that the "Five Thousand" were originally intended to be a much more select body than the zeugites, and that even later the term was not widened to include all of them, but only such as actually possessed hoplite equipment. By this stage of the war many zeugites must have been greatly impoverished and unable to replace their armour.

To summarise the above argument, I would maintain that the figures given by Thucydides and the other ancient authorities are credible. They indicate that during the Pentecontaetia, and especially in its latter half, the numbers of the hoplite class rose rapidly, increasing from about 10,000 at the time of the Persian war to well over 20,000 at the beginning of the Peloponnesian war. They also indicate that the population as a whole must have grown at a prodigious rate. Here no precise figures can be given, but despite the emigration of many thousands of Athenians to colonies, the number of citizens seems to have increased very substantially. Both these movements were the result of a great increase in the national income of the Athenian people, due in part to the expansion of trade and industry, in part to the intensive exploitation of the silver mines, but mainly to the income, distributed in wages, from the Empire, and the acquisition of land in the Empire, privately by purchase or mortgage, and publicly in colonies and cleruchies. This increase in wealth meant both that larger families survived and the population thus expanded, and that a larger proportion of citizens qualified as hoplites; the second movement was probably accentuated by the drop in the real value of the hoplite census caused by rising prices.

During the thirty years of the Peloponnesian war there seems to have been as sharp a fall both in the hoplite class and, though here again no figures are available, in the population generally. This was due to some extent to heavy war casualties, but more to the Plague: for the former would in normal circumstances have had little permanent effect, but the latter, through the presumably heavy mortality among children, would have brought about a lasting decrease. Probably as important as, if not more important than, these factors, however, was the fall in prosperity, due to the devastation of Attica, the decline of productive industry and trade, and in the later stages of the war, the closing of the silver mines, and the loss of imperial revenue and of landed property overseas. These factors would have both reduced many hoplites to thetic status, and have checked the recovery of the population in general. The full effect of the closing of the silver mines and the loss of the imperial revenue and overseas possessions would not have been felt till after the end of the war, when the population seems to have sunk to a figure below what it had reached in the early fifth century.

INDEX OF PASSAGES CITED

LITERARY AUTHORITIES

GENERAL INDEX